Kinship with the Wolf

The Amazing Story of the Woman Who Lives with Wolves

Tanja Askani

Kinship
with the Wolf

The Amazing Story of the
Woman Who Lives with Wolves

Photographs by Sabine Lutzmann
Translated from the German by Douglas Hayes

Park Street Press
Rochester, Vermont

Contents

Park Street Press
One Park Street
Rochester, Vermont 05767
www.ParkStPress.com

Park Street Press is a division of Inner Traditions
International

Library of Congress Cataloging-in-Publication Data
Askani, Tanja.
  [Wolfsspuren. English]
  Kinship with the wolf : the amazing story of the woman
who lives with wolves / Tanja Askani ; photographs
by Sabine Lutzmann ; translated from the German by
Douglas Hayes.
    p. cm.
  ISBN-13: 978-1-59477-130-9 (pbk.)
  ISBN-10: 1-59477-130-8 (pbk.)
  1. Wolves—Germany—Naturschutzgebiet Lüneburger
Heide—Anecdotes. 2. Human-animal relationships—
Germany—Naturschutzgebiet Lüneburger Heide—
Anecdotes . 3. Askani, Tanja. I. Title.
  QL737.C22A7913 2006
  599.773—dc22
                                    2006015709

Printed and bound in India by Replika Press Pvt. Ltd.

10 9 8 7 6 5 4 3 2 1

Text layout by Priscilla Baker
This book was typeset in Janson, with Thesis used as a
display typeface

Foreword

A new era has begun in the history of the relationship between humans and wolves. We have recently become aware of what we have lost through the extinction of so many wild creatures. As a Native American elder said: "If the beasts are gone, we will die of loneliness of spirit." Or, to use a modern notion, we will be destroyed by depression.

What we persecute and exterminate in the outer world, we also eradicate in our souls. We pay for everything that we take away from nature with a loss of vitality, understanding, wisdom, and our sense of security in the world. As a result of our struggle against all wild things, we humans have triggered an unprecedented chain reaction of destruction of the physical world and our own nature and intelligence.

Until recently, animals only had worth to people if they had a "practical" use, beginning with food and continuing through military use and scientific research into their "interesting" DNA.

With the writings of Konrad Lorenz,* a new, authentic interest in animals themselves began. The first generation of wolf biologists followed their curiosity's lead and carried out objective and neutral behavioral research on wolves. In the light of this research, the legend of the wolf's viciousness waned. There slowly developed a picture of a highly intelligent, social, and sensitive creature, a creature at the top of the food chain with an inestimable value for healthy forests and natural systems as a whole. But wolf research took place at a safe distance. The use of numbers and statistics does not allow any relationship between researchers and the focus of their study. The animal remains an "object."

The next generation of wolf researchers began to conduct their work on the basis of their immediate contact with wolves. While this was an important step forward in the relationship between people and wolves, these new researchers measured their success by how much the wolf pack "obeyed" them and the wolves "followed" them. The wolf was still seen as a predator who could only be ruled through the incessant demonstration

---

*Konrad Lorenz was an Austrian ethologist who focused on the study of instinctive behavior in animals. His popular works *King Solomon's Ring* (1952) and *On Aggression* (1966) brought ethology to the attention of the general public and are still widely read today. Lorenz shared the 1973 Nobel Prize in Physiology or Medicine with two other early ethologists.

of human superiority and dominance. The only way we humans could get close to wolves was to continually enforce our power over them.

Tanja Askani has opened the door to a new dimension of relating to wolves. Basing her work on broad respect and profound knowledge, as well as steadfast presence and great love, she has managed to give the interplay between human and wolf a completely new form. In this moving book, she allows us to take part in the way she treats her wolves and what she experiences with them.

When we watch her working with wolves, we can imagine what a friendly, cooperative partnership with these wild creatures might have looked like in earlier times. Simultaneously, her work points to the future. In a very modern way, Tanja Askani lives out the old myth of "Brother Wolf" that has directed human relations with wolves for millennia.

With her extraordinary ability to empathize, she is deeply connected to animals. She is sensitive to wolves' changing feelings and impartially absorbs their moods. Through her remarkable knowledge, she puts wolves' behavior and feelings in a context that is comprehensible even to people who are unfamiliar with these animals. She speaks with her wolves in both wolf and human language, and the wolves respond to her. They come when they are called—out of love and free will, not obedience. She never imposes her will on the wolves unnecessarily. And it is fascinating that she never tries to manipulate them with food; nor does she attempt to foist her wishes on them with other tricks. When a wolf shows aggression, it is just as natural as when it expresses love or affection. Through Askani, we learn that along with love, thoughtfulness, and tenderness, aggression is one of a wolf's natural behaviors, although we cannot justify it when we impose standards of human ethics on the animal. Both romanticizing and demonizing wolves result from human ideals that obstruct our view of reality and hinder true understanding. The author teaches us to accept the animals and their behaviors as they are, free from moral judgments and romantic prejudices.

Her respect for the wolf pack's autonomous rules, which set boundaries for people, is also impressive. She values the rules of the pack more

highly than the human desire to participate and influence. In this way, she also clearly distinguishes herself from other people who work with wolves.

As a child, Tanja Askani already had an intense connection to animals. Her father frequently brought abandoned, sick, or "unnecessary" animals home and cared for them until a new home could be found. But anyone imagining a romantic home in the woods is mistaken. At that time, her family lived in an industrial city in the Czech coalfields. The meadow where four-year-old Tanja kept watch over abandoned lamb triplets was the available green space between skyscrapers. The fox kit the five-year-old girl romped about with was injured by heavy machinery. She spent entire days with the animals of small traveling circuses that came to her city. She fed the ponies and dreamed of working one day with "wild animals" like those belonging to the circus people she admired. But she had mixed feelings about the tricks and coercion that trainers necessarily practiced on the animals.

When Tanja was sixteen years old, people concerned about animal welfare in the city of Novy Jicin founded an injured bird sanctuary. Injured birds were rehabilitated there and later reintroduced to the wild.

Tanja joined this initiative and spent all her time after school there. It was there that she became a falconer.

After finishing school, Tanja studied animal science. Her subsequent job experience was depressing. She was responsible for all the livestock of a huge agricultural cooperative and had to experience the low level of animal care in factory farming. Despite her great dedication, she could accomplish little improvement due to uninterested animal keepers and a merciless, exploitative system. She had responsibility but no influence and finally left in frustration. Nevertheless, her education and her extensive knowledge of biology, physiology, and ethology provided a basis for her later work with wolves.

Tanja had also completed an artistic education, which enabled her to work as a restorer in various museums after she left the agricultural cooperative. Through her artistic work, she developed abilities that would serve her years later in her interaction with wolves: she learned to grasp the world by careful and precise observation, discerning the finest details and understanding their context in a total picture.

For a long time, the idea of devoting herself to wolves was only a dream. As a little girl, Tanja received a book about wolves from her father, and images of these wild creatures were embedded in her soul forever. Decades later, long after she had built a falconry with her husband at the Lüneburger Heide Wild Game Park, she remembered her childhood dream. It happened the moment she first held a newborn wolf pup in her hands—it was Flocke, whom you will meet here. From her old dream came a plan. In this book she allows us to take part in the many wonderful stories that grew from that plan and its realization.

The message of her work, however, reaches far beyond the world of direct contact with wolves and research into their behavior. The kind of relationship that she has developed with wolves is a model of how we can respond to the intelligent complexity of life with care, respect, and wisdom while maintaining an intensive connection to it. She teaches us that contact and relationship with wild animals is possible without human dominance. She teaches us respect for the higher laws dictated by the social structure of nature and how, by recognizing these limits, brand new possibilities for connection can arise.

Through her work Tanja Askani embodies a new, forward-looking ethic of relationship that does not view our associations with wolves as a burden. It is an ethic we urgently need to embrace to redefine our relationships with the natural world. Her work is a wonderful gift to our time.

Rosemarie Kirschmann

Living with Wolves

The tundra wolf's coat insulates so well that snow doesn't melt on it.

Tundra wolves' true element is snow.

January

I am leaning against an old spruce tree, my cold hands dug deep in my pockets. The air smells of frost and fir needles. Snowflakes gently fall and melt on my face. Without moving, I observe how the wolves play around me, scrapping and charging. Fascinated, I watch their clear and genuine presence. The wolf: symbol of the deep, secluded shadowlands of our being; symbol of strength, independence, and wildness. I should go soon, but I simply cannot tear myself away, cannot separate myself from their gaze. They are full of power, but at the same time elegant and sleek, careful and thoughtful, uncompromising and commanding. They appear peaceful and playful, loving and sometimes cuddly, and simultaneously unrestrained and untamably wild. There are so many supposedly irreconcilable characteristics in a wolf.

I observe them very carefully. Every look, every movement has a meaning. This silent wolf language cannot be compared to dog language. Wolf language can be more subtle and exact. A wolf can communicate his feelings, emotions, moods, and intentions with only a facial expression or look. This level of communication is very different from a dog's, with his varied barking and yapping.

Since I am with the wolves not only physically but also with all my senses and my soul, I can recognize signals that would probably remain hidden from an outside observer. Through living with wolves I have learned to decode their highly sophisticated language. I have come to

A human among wolves: only mutual trust between the animals and the author makes this extraordinary closeness possible.

know that reading books and observing from a distance are not enough to build a deep understanding of wolves and their language. With you, my readers, I would like to share my inner connection with wolves.

◼ A Human among Wolves

My perfect world is in the presence of wolves. The day-to-day world remains far away. Here I forget all worries. The stress of everyday life is set aside for later. Here with the wolves—where a respectful, almost religious peace prevails—I feel healthy. I am one of them, bound to them and subject to their laws.

Of course, all three of the wolves know that I am not a real wolf. I would be underestimating their intelligence if I thought I could convince them that I am. But through our close relationship, I am integrated into

their lives. Depending on the situation, they perceive me as a pal, a pack member, or sometimes as competition. They show strong emotional ties.

An interesting experiment allowed me to experience how different the wolves' reactions to me can be under various conditions. A professor who has studied ancient hunting techniques for years carried out this experiment with us at the Lüneburger Heide Wild Game Park. It tests how, for example, aurochs, elk, or red deer react when a person dressed as a predator or ungulate tries to get close to them as did our ancestors, the Ice Age hunters and later primitive people, camouflaged with animal skins. For this purpose, the professor brings a variety of prepared skins. Out of curiosity, I borrow a deer skin, pull it over my head, and crawl on all fours into the wolf enclosure. Although all three wolves immediately recognize me, this costume engenders a brand new behavior toward me. Instead of greeting me, they run somewhat cautiously in a circle around me, remaining a safe five yards away. As soon as I lower the antlers on my head the way a deer does to defend itself, the wolves immediately jump back and distance themselves from me further.

A basic wolf instinct is awakened. Although they were born in captivity, they immediately recognize that antlers can be deadly weapons. Their instinctive knowledge that lowered antlers can lead to danger is stronger than their knowledge that I am hidden under the deer skin. This inborn caution dwells far deeper in their blood than does their certainty that I am not a deer at all. As I stand up, the wolves immediately jump toward me and curiously observe the skin. My upright position is their signal that the "deer danger" is over. To save the skin, I have to flee the enclosure quickly.

After this experience, I cannot resist more experiments, and I borrow a wolf skin. My tension is so thick, it is almost a test of my courage. How will the wolves react now? Will they see in me an unfamiliar wolf, an intruder? With the wolf skin on my back, I crawl into the enclosure and they immediately come racing up to me. But instead of an attack, a storm of wolf greeting awaits me. They nudge me with their noses, lick my face under the wolf mask, wag their tails furiously, and leap with joy. Their overfriendly and obsequious gestures toward me go on endlessly, as if they want to tell me, "Finally, you look like one of us!"

Shared howling strengthens the cohesion of human and wolf.

I am normally entitled to such a greeting ritual only at the beginning of a visit with my wolves. Since I have been in the enclosure for over half an hour and they have already greeted me as a person, my wolf appearance must be something very special for them.

■ Mating Season

The evening sun sinks below the horizon. Fine snowflakes fall gently but incessantly until they have gradually covered all the tracks. It is getting colder. I am still standing motionless under the old spruce, and my hands search deep in my pockets for some warmth. Meanwhile, I never let the wolves out of my sight, and my thoughts are with them.

Today I pay more attention than usual to my female wolf, Flocke [Snowflake]. She stays closer to me than usual, too, as if she senses that a difficult time lies ahead of us. From time to time she jumps up on me and lays her paws on my shoulder, nudging me with her nose, licking my face lightly, and gently chewing on my ear. Then she falls on all fours again and braces her back straight against my legs. I tickle her between the ears, and she enjoys my affection with half-closed eyes.

It is the end of January, the brink of mating season. The days are getting longer, and the growing light encourages the production of sex hormones that trigger the mating instinct. The effect of these

During the mating season, the partners are almost inseparable.

hormones—which are distributed in tiny amounts by the blood—is powerful: mating season begins. And I know that for this reason, starting perhaps tomorrow, I will no longer be able to enter the wolf enclosure. Flocke will follow her instinct, the one that tells her that only the pack's two best and strongest will be allowed to care for offspring.

Nature has apparently furnished a number of control mechanisms. Only the alpha female and alpha male will mate during this period, and they simultaneously prevent any other pack member from mating. The reason for this is very simple. If more than one female gave birth at any given time in a wild pack of wolves, it would be impossible to feed all the pups, and their chances of living to adulthood would be reduced. So a wolf pack requires a form of "birth control." Generally, only the two highest-ranking wolves are allowed to mate, though it does happen that in exceptional cases two female wolves give birth. Most often, these cases involve an alpha female and one of her daughters. This has, in fact, happened here in the game park, when two timber wolf females gave birth at the same time. Immediately after the birth, however, the alpha female took all the pups and raised them herself. Their birth mother could only watch helplessly.

The right of the strongest to reproduce is not unimportant. The offspring of the hardiest parents have the best genetic prerequisites for survival, so only one litter enters the world. But the pups are then loved and pampered, fed and defended, by all pack members.

During the mating season, many tensions and conflicts arise in the pack, stemming from the female wolves' desire to prevent other females from breeding to increase the odds that their own pups will survive. The alpha female is especially ill humored during this time.

The utter terror and stress she inflicts on the other, humbled females is so great that they do not even go into heat at first. I am very close to Flocke, too close to be spared from these conflicts in the pack. For this reason, I have to leave my wolves alone for about four weeks. This is the only way I can prevent a confrontation between Flocke and myself. I respect this, even when it is not easy for me.

One look into the neighboring timber wolf enclosure during the mating season proves to me that this behavior is totally natural. There the alpha female energetically makes it known who is allowed to participate in the "honeymoon" and who is not. There is loud growling and timid whimpering. Wild chases end with the alpha female's dominating gestures and the unmistakably submissive gestures of the lesser female.

Although I have read that the alpha female does not fundamentally object to also mating with the second male in line, I have often observed that our timber wolf alpha female has a clear concept of who her partner should be. The subordinate male took advantage of the alpha male's inattentiveness many times, but he never mated successfully. At first, the alpha female reacted to his attempts to get close to her with play, but as it became serious, she immediately went into a defensive position. This usually ended with submis-

Opposite: An exchange of tenderness.

Above: During the mating season, wolves howl during the day.

sive gestures from the male and a hint at a bite on the throat from the alpha female, accompanied by loud growls and fearful whimpers.

■ Life in the Pack

In the wild, a wolf pack consists of two or three generations, typically a pair of parents and young wolves from the previous year. In such a family group, the roles are clearly divided; the dominant sexually mature pair automatically has the highest place in the hierarchy of the pack. In contrast, almost all wolf packs in captivity consist of older animals who inevitably live together for years, which is only possible through heated power struggles. For this reason, the mating season among captive wolves involves more visible aggression than that among wild wolves. The ritual repeats itself every year at this time. Afterward, however, everything is as it was before; peace reigns again.

I have often been advised to violently assert myself with my wolves to enforce my position in the pack—but exactly what position is that? Why should I show the wolves who is the strongest here and who has the final word? A pack member has not only rights but also obligations. The underlying premise would then be that I am with my pack all day taking part in everyday life. If I am not in a position to fulfill this easiest premise, then I cannot ask about rights. I believe that I have no right to integrate myself so strongly in the life of the pack. Why should I show an alpha female that I am the strongest? She is certainly the one entitled to this position. She has struggled for this place in the pack and earned it; she should also retain it. What would be the sense of asserting myself during the mating season and muddling the entire pack structure? If I did so only because I felt hurt—as the "lord of creation" without respect for other creatures—by the wolves' natural behavior it would be pure egotism. I am convinced that such behavior on my part would conclusively destroy my special relationship with Flocke. Our communion is not only built on mutual love, trust, and understanding but especially on mutual respect, my respect for a wonderful creature. It requires a great deal of sensitivity to know how far you can go and what you can allow yourself without violating the laws of nature. If I were to interfere, I would temporarily destroy Flocke's position in the pack and force her to continually reassert herself to regain her top position due to the natural urge to be the best and show it. After such a clash, Flocke probably would wait until she found a weak spot in me later, which she could exploit to prove herself again to her pack. And that would surely work; a person certainly has plenty of weak spots.

Opposite: Seriously intended attacks can occur without prior warning.

There is no model for how a human should behave in relation to wolves. We must not forget that every wolf is unique and has a strong personality and individuality, with its own special strengths, weaknesses, and character. These differences between individual wolves make it possible for them to create a perfect community. For example, one wolf can smell more acutely than others and so is better able to find prey. Another has more stamina and can pursue prey the longest once it is discovered. A third wolf is an especially experienced hunter and can successfully ambush the prey. There are curious, resourceful, reserved, and shy wolves, and wolves with a great ability to assert themselves. The various mentalities of the pack members serve the purpose of forming a functioning community. Every wolf—with its own character, traits, and experiences—is like a piece of a puzzle. Only together, with all of their weaknesses and strengths, can wolves create a harmonious community capable of surviving: a wolf pack in which every member has its job according to the pack hierarchy.

They all have four basic needs in common, however. They all must have the possibility to fulfill their enormous sense of commitment to family and sense of belonging. This could be called their need for love. They also need freedom. As individuals, they must all have the opportunity

to make independent decisions. The third need is the urge for recognition. To be affirmed by other pack members has great meaning for wolves. Finally, play is no less important. Through play, tensions are reduced in the pack, cohesion is strengthened, and young animals learn what is important in life. These basic needs are the same in humans and wolves, as they are in all intelligent creatures. They only differ in the form of their development and the ways they are realized.

It is getting dark, and my feet begin to feel like icicles. The park has emptied of people. I hear the last visitor's car leave the parking lot. The sound of the motor becomes less and less audible until it eventually fades into the distance. Stillness returns.

All three wolves stand close together and sniff the frosty air once more with their heads held high. Then, in the middle of the enclosure, they roll together back to back in the fresh snow and rest. The snowflakes keep falling, blanketing the sleeping wolves until their bodies disappear into their snowy surroundings. Their thick winter coats keep the warmth from escaping them, so the snow covering their bodies does not melt. I stay with them awhile until I can finally detach myself and go.

Flocke

The history of wolves on earth began more than fifteen million years ago. At that time, the relatively small predator *Tomarctus* developed into the progenitor of the canine family, to which dogs, foxes, coyotes, jackals, and wolves all belong.

■ Rearing a Wolf Pup

My personal history with wolves is considerably shorter. It begins on the day that my husband unexpectedly comes home with an orphaned, hypothermic, three-day-old wolf pup. In the wolf enclosure of the game park where we work, an animal tragedy has taken place. The pup's two siblings and her mother died shortly after their birth, and the only survivor is the little female. Since she is so tiny and light and will one day get a white coat, we name this ball of wool Flocke. Then a battle for her survival begins. The wolf's mother must have been long dead, because the pup is so weak that she doesn't even have her reflex to suck. As I lift her naked skin, it remains standing like a piece of folded paper. This means that her body is totally dehydrated from lack of nutrients. I keep trying to feed her a few drops of dog milk formula. This works, but shortly afterward I determine that the little pup isn't digesting the milk substitute. She has diarrhea, which is life-threatening for her in this situation.

Hour after hour, I massage the little body to stimulate digestion and circulation. I give the pup electrolytes, vitamins, and injections of nutrients. Despite all this, she gets weaker and weaker. As I despondently take this to mean that she will die under my care, I notice that our hunting dog Senta is producing milk, although she has no pups of her own. Dogs inherited this capability from their ancestors, the wolves. In wild wolf packs, generally only the alpha female has pups. If a mother wolf dies, another wolf from the pack takes her role and cares for the young ones. In this way, the survival of the species is secured.

▪ A Dog as Foster Mother

Senta is now Flocke's last chance. I milk the dog drop by drop and give the milk to the baby wolf with a pipette. I know that I cannot burden the pup's weak stomach too much, so she only gets a tiny amount at a time. For Flocke to get her necessary daily ration, I feed her every half hour, so I spend two days and nights switching between milking the dog and feeding the wolf pup. Soon the first successes are apparent. Slowly, Flocke wakes from her lethargy. Her diarrhea disappears and her reflex to suck returns. With my help, she can now nurse directly from the dog, and I weigh her after every nursing to keep watch over the amount of

For all young animals, play is preparation for life.

nutrients she consumes. Senta patiently tolerates everything. But when I push the pup in front of her snout, she turns away. Senta has never had her own pups. Despite the fact that she is producing milk, she has not begun to have maternal feelings. Not even sprinkling the young wolf with Senta's milk persuades her. A few days later, a positive change finally takes place. I am sitting with the dog and the pup on the floor, as I often do these days, to assist Flocke with nursing. The baby wolf falls on her side with her full belly and begins to whimper loudly. Suddenly Senta curls up. The dog raises her ears and cautiously sniffs the little one. As Flocke whimpers again, it happens. Senta's maternal feelings awaken. She pushes her belly forcefully to the pup and licks Flocke so intensely that I fear Senta will suffocate her. I spend the next night on the floor with both of them to make sure everything is okay. Soon I am convinced: Senta has finally decided to adopt the wolf pup. From this day on, she never leaves the pup's side. Senta is with the pup around the clock; she nurses her, protects and warms her, licks and cleans her. This is very welcome for me, because Senta takes over a large share of my worries. Under her supervision, Flocke makes great progress; she grows so fast you can almost see it.

Compared to dogs, wolves develop unbelievably fast. In just six months, wolf pups reach the size of an adult wolf, with good reason: Born in the spring, they must accompany the pack in all its travels by fall.

In contrast, a dog in the care of people can take time to grow up. Dogs do not face the hard test of winter; their life conditions are independent of the seasons. Without hunger, long journeys, or other strains, dogs can allow themselves the luxury of taking up to three years to develop fully. Their masters ensure that all of their needs are met.

As a result of domestication, since they do not have to defend their young against the forces of wild nature, dogs can theoretically have pups twice a year. Wolves have their pups only in spring, when the best conditions for rearing them occur. Dogs are capable of reproducing at a much younger age than wolves. Dogs are sexually mature at seven to eight months old; wolves, in contrast, must wait at least two years for their sexual maturity, when they have already long resembled adults in appearance.

■ The Unruly Instinct to Play

Our wolf pup is growing rapidly. Her coat gets lighter every day, her legs longer. Her head slowly takes on the form of a wolf's, and her movements become more lithe. She continually gets stronger and more active. Like a small child, Flocke needs the supervision of an adult to prevent her from injuring herself while playing. She plays with everything that appears in front of her nose. In this way, she learns what is important for her future life as a wolf: attack and defense, assertiveness and submission. With Flocke's growing abilities, our whole house inevitably changes. Soon she rules the ground floor. We move the houseplants to a height that will save them, and the flower vases, flatware, and other "toys" must be put out of the way of the young wolf. Everything that Flocke can get a grip on carries the unmistakable marks of her teeth. To punish her for this makes no sense, since her teeth are her most important means of exploring her environment. In the wild, a healthy and lively pup is the pride of the whole wolf pack. Therefore, she would never understand if she were to be punished for her natural urge to play.

To live with a wolf means constant new surprises and challenges. A short lapse of attention on our part results in all the chewable materials of our brand new bicycle being dismantled in less than fifteen minutes, from the saddle to the cable to the tires. The young wolf also leaves her

Opposite above: Walks outside of the enclosure are Flocke's greatest joy.

Opposite below: Flocke returns to the enclosure a little exhausted but content.

conspicuous tracks in our yard, where she apparently has her own ideas about landscaping. The lawn is quickly riddled with deep holes that she digs to hide her treasures in. Every movement of a blade of grass or a flower petal is an invitation for her to play. She persistently stalks tufts of grass, jumps on them, snatches them, and shakes them like prey. And so she transforms our once-green yard into a desert.

After the Japanese carp in our pond awaken Flocke's hunting instinct, we are persuaded to create a safe zone with an electric fence. In the meantime, she begins spending nights outside. She never uses the dog-house intended for her, preferring instead to sleep in the middle of the yard under the open sky. From there, she can carefully follow the events behind the wooden fence or in the house.

At some point our wolf has taught herself to open the door to the house, and one night she enters and destroys the ground floor while we are sleeping. Thereafter, we put up electric wires on the door, as well as on the windows and the gate to the yard. Gradually, our property begins to resemble an impenetrable fortress.

From the beginning, it is clear to us that Flocke cannot stay with us forever. Although the wolf is the ancestor of the dog, the two have only a few things in common. Over generations, dogs have grown dependent on people and favor them as companions. Wolves, in contrast, do not need to be with people to survive and prefer to be with their own kind. Not even Flocke's adopted mother, Senta, could permanently replace a wolf pack. To give Flocke the best possible preparation for her future life as a wolf, I take her with me to the game park every day. She will live there later, and I would like her to get used to the visitors and the strange smells and noises while she is still a pup.

Our short car ride becomes torturous with time. Flocke immediately learns to move lightning-fast over the car seats. With her powerful teeth and sharp claws, she destroys the carpet, the seatbelts, and the plastic window seals. With great persistence, she tries to bite off everything protruding from the dashboard. This seems much more interesting to her at the moment than the toys and cow bones that I bring along as distractions during the drive. I have to fasten Flocke to

the back seat of the car to be able to drive relatively safely.

Every afternoon I go walking with Senta and Flocke for a couple of hours. On the short path through the village, Flocke must stay on her leash because there are chickens, geese, and cats there, and I know that when wolves are overcome with curiosity and the fever of the hunt they can no longer be called back. Besides, the traffic could be dangerous for her.

I only let Flocke run off the leash in the woods. Here she can fully enjoy her freedom. On hot days, especially, she jumps out in front to be the first to the marshy bank of the river, where she loves to splash in the shallow water. Even after she has played for a long time, she will not leave the river to follow me further. In the woods, we frequently meet walkers, mushroom gatherers, or horseback riders. A wild wolf would make a big arc around every person. Not our Flocke. Once I have to drag her off a picnic blanket. Another time she comes to me with a pillow between her teeth. The jogger whose shorts Flocke playfully tries to take down is not thrilled with this encounter. Fortunately, it does not occur to anyone Flocke meets that this little pup could be a wolf.

So the summer flies by, and the day that Flocke leaves us to move into her enclosure draws nearer. Over these two months, the wolf has grown very dear to our hearts. Our whole family struggles to hold back tears during her move, but none of us want to deny her the right to live the life of a wolf.

■ From a Human Family to Wolf Society

From now on, Flocke shares her new home with Prinz [Prince], a young male wolf from the Berlin Zoo. Prinz has grown up in a wolf pack and is not influenced by people. A close relationship between a wolf and a human such as the one Flocke and I share can only develop when a human takes a wolf away from its mother at a very young age and lets it grow up with people. Although Prinz was born in captivity and is familiar with visitors and caretakers, an invisible barrier remains between him and humans. After a short time, curiosity drives him to trust me enough to come within a few yards of me. As soon as I move, however, his inborn fear and respect for people win out, and he flees with his tail between his legs to the farthest corner of the enclosure.

Although Flocke and Prinz befriend each other quickly, my female wolf appears to greatly miss our previous intensive contact. Every time I visit her in the enclosure, she greets me so forcefully that afterward I am happy to find that my ears and nose remain unharmed. She jumps up on me with full force to greet me with a wolf "kiss." When she hits my face, it feels like I am standing in a boxing ring being knocked out by my opponent. Afterward, I try to prevent the other visitors from noticing my bleeding nose by discreetly wiping it with a Kleenex. When you come out of a wolf enclosure smeared with blood, it is difficult to explain that this is only proof of a wolf's love. Prinz stands behind a tree and watches everything from a safe distance. Evidently, he cannot understand Flocke's excitement.

Sometimes I put Senta and Flocke on a leash and we take a walk together as we did in the old days. Each time the young wolf wildly greets the dog. She whimpers and licks Senta's snout, wags her tail vigorously, and jumps for joy around the dog. With bent legs and friendly, flattened ears, Flocke shrinks and shows the dog her obsequiousness and devotion. This outpouring of happiness to see Senta again appears to make the dog rather uncomfortable. She growls quietly at Flocke and pushes away her attempts to get closer. But Senta's threatening gestures do not deter the wolf. Instead, Flocke tries to express her submissiveness even more clearly.

Flocke in her element.

We start running. It takes about ten minutes to reach the area outside the park where I let them run free—Flocke's greatest joy.

From a distance, I hear the desperate howling of Flocke's abandoned companion, Prinz, in his enclosure. In human language, the howling means: "Flocke, where are you? If you hear me, give me an answer!" Although Flocke and Prinz get along well, she never answers him. "A traitor," I think to myself. Though she must be able to hear him, she doesn't look once in his direction. She is simply happy in this moment that she does not have to be where he is, locked up in an enclosure. She longs for movement and space. She enjoys her freedom, romps endlessly, jumps behind Senta, and rolls in any garbage that emits a special "wolf perfume." Most of the time, she remains within sight of me. If she goes a little farther away, however, my dog whistle is sufficient to call her back. Flocke notices very quickly that Senta turns around and runs to me after a single whistle. And thus Flocke is usually by my side faster than the dog. Not because she obeys so well, but because she is curious to know why Senta hurries to me so fast.

■ The Instinct to Hunt

In the area outside the park, there are many fishponds. On one of the pond's banks, the fish farmers have built a garden shed. Soon Flocke discovers that she will always find something to play with there. Just off the leash, she runs back with work gloves, a garden hose, a plastic tub, or a rubber boot.

Once, as Senta catches sight of a pair of ducks on one of the ponds, she jumps into the water like the hunting dog she is and swims after the ducks with excited barks. The ducks take it easy and paddle calmly to the opposite bank. Though Flocke has never hunted in a wolf pack, she reacts like a wolf immediately. She dashes quietly ahead to surprise the ducks on the other side of the pond. It does not occur to her that they can fly!

Flocke has also discovered another form of entertainment. Not far beyond the ponds lives a small population of wild rabbits. Is there anything nicer than hunting down a rabbit? The first time I catch Flocke noticing one of these fleeing animals, the shock goes right through me: now she will certainly run after it. And that is what she does. But not even a minute passes before she returns, somewhat disappointed. The experienced rabbit has shaken Flocke off quickly and has probably disappeared into the first burrow.

We run back to the park. Flocke goes more and more slowly over the last hundred yards. Her companion Prinz notices her from a distance. He whimpers happily, wags his tail, and jumps excitedly along the enclosure's fence. But this proof of love leaves Flocke cold; she does not once look in his direction. Instead, she sniffs each square inch of earth, each blade of grass, each branch, cleverly trying to avoid the way that leads back to her enclosure.

With time, she will learn that this is her home and that human society cannot replace life in the wolf pack.

Chinook

One day a tragic accident happens in the enclosure. Prinz breaks a leg joint while playing. The injury is so severe that we cannot do anything more for him and must put him to sleep. Along with mourning over the young wolf comes the dilemma of what should happen now with Flocke. For the first time in her life, she is alone, a situation that we have tried to prevent all along. Is there anything worse for a wolf than loneliness?

Opposite: At a full run, a wolf can achieve speeds of up to 35 miles per hour.

Chinook curiously, but always cautiously, surveys his new surroundings.

We have to find a suitable new companion for Flocke, and quickly. But since only a few German game parks own tundra wolves, the odds are slim. Nevertheless, fate lends a hand. I hear that a no-less-sad event has happened recently in Bavaria. There, an acquaintance has kept a pair of tame tundra wolves in an enclosure for years. The female wolf escaped and was shot by the police. I call my acquaintance and ask what his plans are for his lone wolf, who creeps as unhappily around his enclosure as our Flocke. Should we bring the two together? He agrees to my proposal.

We leave immediately, and a couple of hours later we have the seven-year-old Chinook in the car, packed in a crate. Bringing two adult animals together is not completely without risk. No one can say ahead of time if the two lone wolves will get along with each other.

■ A New Wolf in the Family

Almost no other mammal has such well-developed social behavior as the wolf. But this does not mean that two unacquainted wolves will accept each other. A "native" wolf in its territory will view an unknown wolf as an intruder and will not tolerate it. If Flocke and Chinook do not get along, we will have to return the male wolf to his owner. Fortunately, Chinook is the quietest, gentlest tundra wolf I have ever seen: a sheep in wolf's clothing! As Flocke—kept on her leash during the two wolves' first contact—bares her teeth, Chinook simply licks her on the nose in a friendly fashion. Thereafter, she behaves peacefully as well. It is hard to believe how quickly the two become friends. On the second day, I see them lying right next to each other in the enclosure.

Chinook is still very distrustful of me and all other people, however. When I enter the enclosure, he maintains a safe distance. During this period, I spend every free minute with the wolves and notice that Chinook, driven by his curiosity, trusts himself to come closer and closer to me. It takes another couple of days until he allows me to touch and pet him.

During this time we refrain, with heavy hearts, from our regular walks with Flocke. We do not want to leave Chinook alone. I put a collar on him several times a day and practice running with him inside the enclosure. Chinook and I will have to get to know each other before we can walk together outside. I must be certain that he completely trusts me and will not react with panic. When animals in confinement feel threatened and have no way to escape, they usually react aggressively. And it is clear which one of us will fare worse if this happens.

Every day, Chinook makes visible progress. I am downright proud of him. It can't be easy for a wolf to leave his accustomed surroundings and arrive in an unfamiliar place with a new caretaker, a new companion, and a completely new daily routine: all of this at his ripe age of seven years.

We start by taking Chinook out of the enclosure in the evenings when the park is empty of people. My daughter Katerina helps me, taking Flocke on one leash while I lead Chinook. Everything goes as well as it can, so we soon decide to take a real walk with both wolves.

■ Enclosure and Freedom

To go walking—that is our wolves' greatest joy! All the tensions that build up in the enclosure over the course of a day disappear. It is clear that the biggest and nicest enclosure cannot replace roaming free. Eventually you know every stone and every blade of grass, and eyeing the visitors all day gets boring. Would you like to remain locked in the living room with your partner your whole life? An enclosure, even when it is spacious, affects a wolf who longs for freedom and space just as a large room would affect us humans. A person can, of course, spend a few cozy hours there but can't live there permanently. Every dog owner also knows this behavior. No matter how big the yard is, the dog eventually has a breakdown. As soon as he sees his master coming with the leash, however, he flies out of the house. Hurray, let's go! Now something's happening! And this need is naturally incomparably larger for a wolf.

During our walks in the park with the wolves, we encounter many families. It is interesting to see that the children and adults always react

Chinook loves running free, and it is difficult to bring him back into the enclosure.

differently. When children notice us, they call out spontaneously, even from a distance: "Look, Mom, that's a real wolf!" This is unimaginable for the parents, and they immediately attempt to enlighten their offspring: "No, dear, it is not a wolf. A wolf does not run on a leash."

Such different reactions are easily explained by the development of the human brain. A preschool-aged child has a more developed right brain than left brain. The right brain is not rational; it is responsible for emotions, intuition, the perception of sounds, music, moods, and impressions. The left side, in contrast, is rational. It controls, among other things, the functions of language and logical thought. Not until the ages six to seven is the left side developed enough to take over most of the physical functions that the right side has controlled until then. From then on, both hemispheres simultaneously register every stimulus, but the rational left hemisphere tends to dominate conscious perception, while the more complex and holistic perceptions of the right brain become more subconscious.

It is well-known that small children have a very different way of seeing than adults do. Their ability to act intuitively and without prejudice allows them, in this case, to immediately recognize the "animal on the leash" as a wolf.

On the way back through the side entrance to the park we have to put both wolves on their leashes. Chinook quickly grasps the connection: being put on the leash means going back to the enclosure. With time, it becomes progressively more difficult to put him on the leash. He doesn't run away, but he remains at a safe distance of about ten feet from me. If I take a step toward him, he immediately takes a step back. If I take a

step back, he comes a step closer. A fantastic game! Finally, I get hold of him. To convince Chinook that this is not a trick to lock him up, we run through the game park. And this actually helps. From then on, we allow time for a walk through the game park after every excursion in the open spaces. As long as I stick to this rule, I have no more problems putting him on the leash.

But Chinook still doesn't want to go back into the enclosure. It helps some to take a different path, but unfortunately this only works the first time. By the second time, he already knows that our new path also leads to the enclosure and notes this for the future. In a short time, he knows all the paths in the park, and it becomes almost impossible to get him back into the enclosure. His unbelievable sense of direction leads to our plan's undoing over and over again. The last hundred yards are the worst; they require nerves of iron. He tries every trick to delay us; he even lies down in the middle of the path and refuses to take another step. Visitors passing by sympathetically ask, "What's wrong with your dog? Is he sick?" How embarrassing! I encourage him, but he closes his eyes as if he wants to say, "I hear nothing more, I see nothing more, and I'm staying here! This is better than letting myself be locked up!" What should you do with a 120-pound wolf who simply lies there motionless? Fetch a wheelbarrow to transport him? He can only be moved to stand up and follow us through goodness and a quiet voice; it takes a great deal of artful persuasion.

One time, I'm in somewhat of a hurry. After we've been walking for at least three hours, Chinook lies down in the middle of the path not a hundred feet from the enclosure. I encourage him, but he lies there and does not react. Then I lose patience. I try to force him to stand up and move on and energetically jerk his leash, as I would with a dog. Chinook lifts his head, flashes his teeth, and growls at me, as if to say, "Up to here and no further! I will not let something like this be done with me, by God!" This is the first and last time that I try to move him this way. The only thing I can do, as in future similar occasions, is encourage Chinook until he eventually gets up and walks on. The final yards take a good half hour.

As I finally lock his enclosure, he leans against the fence and looks me

Wolf partner test: Flocke takes the prey from Chinook and forces him to prove that he can take care of her and future offspring.

reproachfully in the eyes, as if to say, "What have I done wrong to make you go away again?" Fear of the enclosure, which for Chinook means being locked up and abandoned, never entirely leaves him.

■ The Foundation of Trust between Human and Wolf

With time, a solid, trusting relationship builds between the wolf pack and me. Chinook, the white giant, develops into a "cuddly" wolf who will not leave my side. Even at feeding time, he ignores his meat and prefers to get a dose of affection from me. Again and again, he also takes other people into his heart, especially women. Thus, I am depressed all the more that he refuses to let my husband Lothar touch him, although Lothar visits and takes care of the wolves in the enclosure almost as often as I do. I can find no explanation for Chinook's mistrust.

It occurs to me at some point that Chinook only accepts people who accompany us on our excursions. I propose to my husband that he attempt to gain acceptance this way. He doubts that Chinook will be impressed by this and maintains that the wolf has no opinion about who walks with him or next to him. He finds a connection between a walk and the creation of trust improbable, and it's difficult to convince him to go along. One afternoon it works, though, and off we go. Chinook runs ahead and is distracted by the many different smells. It appears that he does not even perceive who is taking part in the walk. But back in the park we notice a change in his behavior. For the first time, Lothar can take Chinook's collar off and scratch him between the ears without the wolf fleeing. I am relieved that my intuition was correct and my plan worked.

The short period of freedom during our walks is enormously important for the wolves, and they project this positive experience onto the people who accompany them. After about a week, though, Chinook's trust in Lothar wanes again, and in this way he persuades my husband to regularly spend afternoons with the wolves off the leash.

◼ Wolf Partner Test

A couple of months pass. In the meantime Chinook has settled in, he and Flocke get along wonderfully, and it appears that nothing can destroy this idyllic situation. So I am all the more frightened when one day, while the wolves are feeding, I observe Flocke behaving aggressively toward Chinook without apparent reason. Although there is plenty of food, Flocke collects all the pieces of meat, carries them to one spot, and guards them. As soon as Chinook nears her to eat, Flocke shoots out and bites him away. What's wrong? There is certainly enough for both of them there. I feel sorry for the hungry Chinook, and to prevent further conflicts, I quickly get another portion of meat from our animal kitchen. Once I'm back in the enclosure, I see Flocke standing with her legs spread over her pile of meat and Chinook circling her, irritated. He doesn't have the courage, however, to get closer to Flocke and her "prey." I call Chinook to me, and, full of sympathy, I stick a juicy piece of meat directly in his mouth. Flocke notices this, though, and before Chinook can begin to eat, she comes to him and rips that piece away as well, with threatening growls. The same thing happens with my second and third tries to feed Chinook. It's almost impossible to look fast enough to see the pieces of meat change owners. My disbelief grows with the mountain of meat between Flocke's legs. Finally, I cut small "goulash pieces" that Chinook can consume at once, without chewing, and give them to him without being noticed.

Only later do I understand what's going on. It has nothing to do with Flocke not being able to tolerate Chinook anymore. It is quite the other way around. Flocke has chosen Chinook as a partner and put him to the test. Using what seemed at first sight unjust behavior, she wants to force Chinook to prove that he can provide for her and their future pups. By taking his food, she compels him to hunt for more. Before mating in the wild, the alpha male is entrusted with finding food. Presumably, such a form of "partner test" takes place among wild wolves, as well.

Over time, based on various situations, I have observed that a relatively strict matriarchy prevails in our pack. The final decision in important matters always belongs to Flocke.

Nanuk

Flocke and Chinook get along outstandingly well, and I very much hope that they will finally have pups. Unfortunately, the wolf pack doesn't exactly appear to be savvy when it comes to mating, and so the den remains empty this spring, to my great disappointment. At nine years old, Chinook is probably getting too old to produce offspring.

After long deliberation, I decide to enlarge our little wolf pack by one member. In case anything should happen to Chinook, Flocke would then have a new companion with whom she is already familiar. I decide to get a young male and raise him on a bottle to get him used to people. In this way it will be easier to integrate the pup into the existing tame pack without fear or shyness.

The second wolf pack, into which Flocke was born a few years ago, has pups again this spring. When they are a week old, the veterinarian checks their health. During their examination, they are wormed, immunized, and marked with electronic chips. We pick the strongest male out of the litter, and his siblings remain in the pack so the female can raise them herself.

We name the little pup Nanuk, which means "polar bear" in the Inuit language. From the beginning, Nanuk is of a totally different caliber from the once deathly ill little Flocke. As a young pup, he has big character differences that can already be distinguished. At four weeks, Nanuk leaves our house and wants to stay in the yard. We install an electric fence to make our property escape-proof. From now on, Nanuk spends the days in the yard; evenings, I shut him on the porch, where he is protected from

Opposite above: For his first walk, Nanuk is no taller than the grass.

Opposite middle: In contrast to Flocke, Nanuk is very loving as a pup.

Opposite below: Not only meat is on Nanuk's menu; he also tries vegetarian food.

the wind and rain. The dog, Senta, avoids him. She wants nothing to do with him. Raising one wolf is enough for one dog's life.

For company, the pup enlists our two-year-old female dachshund Drossel day and night. Nanuk is five weeks old and exactly the right size for Drossel. They romp and play around the clock; to sleep, they lie crowded together in the dog basket. Nanuk continues to receive his little bottle from me. Once, when he spits out a handful of dachshund hair after drinking his milk, it becomes clear to me how brave Drossel must be when they play. In less than two weeks the dog saves herself from Nanuk on the safe height of the table in the yard.

It is interesting that the little wolf doesn't show any aggression toward me at this age as Flocke did. Thus my earlier supposition is confirmed. With Flocke, the dog Senta took on the role of mother. She protected and nursed the little wolf around the clock. Since I was constantly nearby, Flocke categorized me as one of her siblings. With Nanuk, I adopt the role of mother, and Drossel is the "wolf sister."

◼ Dietary Habits

At five to six weeks old, wolf pups begin to eat meat, and jealousy over food develops. At the same time, they begin violent hierarchy struggles, which I also clearly got a taste of with Flocke. At exactly this age, she began to have competitive battles with me. Although she was only the size of a cat, her behavior made it clear that she meant business. She growled at me while wrinkling her nose and tried to snap at my fingers. She only

Wolves do not understand jokes while they are eating and defend their food by growling.

Wolves can be very good swimmers if they are introduced to water early.

gave up when I behaved exactly as she did. Since I am the mother in Nanuk's eyes this time, I am spared such disputes.

Right on schedule at six weeks, Nanuk refuses milk for the first and last time. From now on, he eats only meat. This surprises me, since I saw Flocke still nursing from Senta at four months old, and with her we also had difficulties with the change to solid food.

I planned ahead for this period and froze juicy portions of deer loin for Nanuk. The little one should only get the best, of course. So I sit with him on the grass in our yard cutting little strips of the tender meat and offering them to him. He takes them without any special enthusiasm and chews away without appetite. I imagined wolf hunger differently! I mention this to my husband, who is standing in our dog run and distributing cow stomachs to the animals. "Try giving him this," he says. Before I can argue, my husband holds the huge, tough, and unpleasant-smelling lobes of a cow stomach in front of Nanuk's nose. Even the sight of this makes me feel nauseous—but not Nanuk. He spits out the chewed-up venison steak lightning fast and bites down on the undefined mass of stomach. Snarling and absolutely determined not to give up his tasty morsel, he carries it to the furthest corner of the yard. From a distance, I see how focused he is on the cow stomach and how he devours the hunk of meat without chewing; it is clear to me that Nanuk has had it with my deer loin.

■ Desire for Freedom

Nanuk grows and develops amazingly fast, as is common with wolf pups. Apparently, he has decided to explore the yard on the other side of the electric fence, too. When I have to retrieve him the first time, I take a long time looking for a hole in the fence. Without success. It is not clear to me how he managed to get past it. Once Flocke became uncomfortably familiar with the electric fence, she fully accepted it. She recognized it as the border of her territory, although she was almost

"Come and catch me!" Nanuk repeatedly thinks up new games.

fully grown and could even have jumped over it without any effort.

Nanuk, with his desire for action, is different. If he gets something in his head, it is impossible to keep him from his plan. After I find him at the other end of the yard and bring him back, in only a few minutes he tries to get through the electric fence again with unbelievable persistence. While he's doing this, he holds his sensitive nose against the ground to protect it from electric shock. The rest of his body is insulated by his thick coat. He tries again and again—the world behind the fence appears so tempting to him.

At two months of age, Nanuk breaks out again and undertakes a longer tour of exploration. I assume that he's just lying in the shade somewhere and sleeping, but my attempts to find him are unsuccessful. I run around and call him increasingly loudly. At last, I see something moving in the nearby meadow at the edge of the woods. No kidding, it's Nanuk! He trots over to me and greets me. His eyes seem to say that he can't understand my excitement.

■ Admission to the Pack

It's actually quite unusual that a little pup would trust itself so far away from its "mother den," but our sterile yard apparently has become too dull for Nanuk. It is now high time to introduce him to the pack. I'm aware that this undertaking is not without danger. If something goes wrong, Nanuk could be killed with a single bite. Tensions can build up among the wolves in the enclosure and it would be possible—though inexplicable to us—for the pack members to react angrily to him.

Both Flocke and Chinook have already gotten to know Nanuk indirectly. Since the pup has lived in our house, they have inspected me very carefully every time I visit their enclosure. Flocke, in particular, sniffs me very intensely every time—concentrating on my hands, my lap, and my shirt—and can hardly tear herself away. What could she be thinking? Indeed, as alpha female, she made very certain during the mating season that no one but she could get pregnant. I had to avoid her, and now I appear with a pup. She probably no longer understands the world.

To prevent every possible risk, the first real meeting is arranged to occur on neutral ground. We go for a walk together. For the experienced Chinook, it's love at first sight. He already had pups once with his earlier partner, so he knows right away what is to be done. He immediately follows Nanuk step by step and never lets him out of his sight. Flocke, in contrast, is somewhat awkward and appears not to know what to do with Nanuk. Her feelings seem mixed. On the one hand, she submits herself to him; on the other, she jumps up immediately and tries to get out of his way when he comes too close to her. We have to take many walks together before I can be certain that Flocke has fully accepted the little one.

In the meantime, to gradually get Nanuk used to the enclosure, I take him there for a couple of hours in the afternoons. Compared to our yard it is a paradise for him: a big pond to splash in, holes to hide in, feathers and bones to play with, and most important of all, two wolves available

Opposite: Nanuk's expression very often shows what is going on inside him.

Howling is wolves' most impressive means of communication.

After six months, Nanuk is almost fully grown.

for every form of entertainment. Despite all of this, at first Nanuk welcomes my return in the late afternoon to pick him up and take him home. He's so tired from playing that he falls asleep in my arms on the way. But it doesn't take much longer before he feels on top of the world in the enclosure. I decide to leave him with his new family.

Nanuk's move into the enclosure positively influences the whole pack. Above all, it causes a wonderful change in Chinook's behavior. There is no trace left of his earlier quiet and heaviness; he pursues the pup energetically and brightly, nibbling or licking Nanuk's coat or trying to get him to play. Flocke and Chinook are busy around the clock teaching the little one to behave like a real wolf, watching out for him, and playing with him. Nanuk fully enjoys their attention. On November 1 he is six months old and, in his first winter coat, almost as big as Chinook. But Nanuk will have to wait a good three years before his coat is Chinook's almost pure white color.

In the meantime, my eleven-year-old hunting dog Senta always accompanies me to the enclosure. She lies in front of the gate and waits patiently until I've taken care of the wolves and come out again. She's not allowed to go in, and since the pack began taking care of Nanuk, Senta can no longer take part in our walks, either. Nanuk could awaken protective instincts in the two adult wolves that could be very dangerous for the dog. For this reason, Flocke and Senta have not had any direct contact for a long time. Nevertheless, Flocke stands against the fence every time, watching the indifferent dog and trying repeatedly to express friendliness and submission through her body language. Flocke still accepts Senta as her mother, but this doesn't mean that they couldn't have differences of opinion. In such a case, the old dog would have no chance; a conflict could be deadly for her.

Waiting for Pups

It is the end of January, the mating season lies ahead, and four-year-old Flocke is at her best age for getting pregnant. With readiness to mate comes a change in behavior, a growing unrest that shows itself weeks ahead of time.

During our walks, Flocke is preoccupied with intensively marking her territory. She marks her scent every ten yards or so on trees, tufts of grass, and other objects. To do this, she either lifts a leg like a male or almost stands on her head to reach the highest and most conspicuous places. Then she paws and scrapes the ground to leave visual markers there as well. No one should fail to notice that this area belongs to her and her pack.

■ Hierarchy Struggles

More than ever, Flocke wants to show everyone that she is the one who has the right to reproduce. She instinctively attempts to drive away any competitors who could threaten her position in the pack. Her behavior toward Senta suddenly changes. Submissiveness becomes dominance; the body language is so clear that it is impossible to overlook the change. Flocke no longer runs along the fence whimpering and wagging her tail with her ears down and legs bent to look as small and friendly as she can. In contrast, when she sees Senta coming she stands sideways and works to impress the dog with the size of her body. She lifts her head and tail up high, puts her ears forward, and raises the hairs on her nape. You almost get the feeling that she is stretching herself like a ballerina on the tips of her toes to more clearly show her authority and size. With stiff legs, Flocke silently follows the dog with her eyes; you can almost feel the growing tension between them. Senta immediately notices Flocke's transformation and turns away from her gaze, holding back growls. She instinctively recognizes that the time for her adopted daughter to go her own way has finally come.

In the wild, too, young wolves do not remain with their parents forever. They gradually separate themselves, making increasingly long

During the mating season, rough-and-tumble games are a permanent part of behavior between partners.

Opposite: Flocke is very temperamental toward others, but not unpredictable.

excursions alone until they eventually break away entirely. With some luck, they find an unoccupied area where they can start a new pack, or they succeed in integrating with an already existing one. On such journeys it is not unusual for wolves to put up to six hundred miles behind them, contributing to their dispersal and reducing the danger of inbreeding.

In the following days, Flocke views me as competition too. She is very moody, but not unpredictable. She now decides every day whether I am allowed in the enclosure to clean or whether I am only allowed to stand outside the fence, and she gives me her decision quickly and clearly. She explicitly conveys all important information to me through her posture.

During serious hierarchy struggles within a pack, however, attacks can arise from a completely neutral posture. Such an attack comes without warning, without such signals as bared teeth, growling, or raised hairs on the nape. Reluctance to bite is abandoned, and there is no possibility

for the loser to submit. These struggles, which mostly occur between two wolves of the same sex, can even lead to fatal injuries. I'm probably only protected from such battles by my respect and reserve toward the wolves.

■ Mating and Pregnancy

For days, I observe that Flocke and Chinook spend much more time together than usual. They play very intensely and show their growing affection with mutual sniffing, nibbling, and licking. Such intense fore-play has the important function of bringing both animals into heat at the same time.

In contrast to a dog, a male wolf is not always fertile. When the ability to take care of offspring only presents itself once a year, uninterrupted readiness to mate would be an unnecessary expenditure of energy. The absence of irritability and competitive behavior that accompanies male wolves' lack of sexual interest during the majority of the year contributes to the social peace of the pack. The scent of a female in heat initiates an increase in a male wolf's testosterone level and causes his otherwise very small testicles to swell to three times their normal size and produce fertile sperm.

During mating season, sexual intercourse is normally repeated several times a day. The male's penis grows so much during intercourse that the partners are not able to uncouple themselves for several minutes. This so-called "hanging" is also common among other doglike animals and guarantees the unhindered transmission of the male's sperm.

Although I spend several hours a day at the wolf enclosure, I never observe Flocke and Chinook mating. I have to come to terms with the fact that this year will not bring our desired offspring to the pack.

The mating season is over in the middle of March, and after this long break we all go for our first walk together again. It strikes us how lovingly and carefully Flocke and Chinook interact. When Flocke stays behind to check out something in the grass, Chinook immediately turns around, runs to her, and worriedly licks her on the nose. He doesn't let Flocke out of his sight for a second. Most of the time, they trot side by side so closely that they touch. They act like a pair of young lovers. Only now do I become convinced that Flocke will, in fact, have pups for the first time.

The pair's behavior is clear, but on the outside Flocke remains unchanged. In mid-April, I still can't distinguish any evidence of a progressing pregnancy by touching her. Finally, at the end of the month, I observe that she is losing the thick coat on her belly. Tundra wolves retain their winter coat for a relatively long time, since winters are very long and summers very short in their native region. The hair on their flanks only begins to mat and fall out in clumps at the end of May. A pregnant wolf's coat changes differently. The hormonal changes caused by the pregnancy result in her losing the hair on her belly first to make her teats accessible to her pups.

At the beginning of May, Flocke disappears more and more often into

Opposite: Chinook and Flocke act very loving with each other and never leave each other's side.

the den that she has dug with Chinook over the past few weeks. It's amazing how easily she passes through the narrow entrance, which is no larger than that of a fox den. No other member of the pack is allowed inside; when, out of curiosity, Nanuk tries to enter, Flocke immediately and energetically chases him away.

One day I notice that Flocke is restlessly pacing back and forth between her den and the back of the enclosure. Chinook greets her every new appearance with humble gestures, which Flocke reacts to nervously, and then she disappears again into her den. When she doesn't appear outside for three days, it gets interesting. There must be a reason for her behavior. Have the pups already been born? If they have, how many are there?

During her pups' first days, every wolf mother stays with them without interruption. So I really have no reason to worry. Nevertheless, curiosity draws me to the den. I kneel in front of the entrance and listen for whimpers or other pup noises, but everything is quiet. Only when I call Flocke by her name does she answer me from the depths with a growl. This does not disturb me, because in the days after giving birth the mother keeps everyone at a distance. The next day, I try again to entice Flocke out of the den, but I'm not successful. Gradually, I become restless. Is everything okay under the ground?

That evening, Flocke appears outside

Flocke disappears into the den she dug herself.

again for the first time. It is immediately apparent that she is not doing well. She can hardly hold herself up, curves her back, shivers, and is in pain. The veterinarian I call immediately decides to do an emergency operation. Flocke receives anesthesia in the enclosure so we can transport her to the clinic. In the fifteen minutes it takes the anesthesia to work, we dig up the den to find her pups. To our disappointment, we discover an empty den about twenty feet down.

The veterinarian's examination reveals that Flocke only carried one pup. It was too big to pass through the birth canal and got stuck in the pelvic area. Our help came too late for the little one; it had probably been dead for several days. The difficult operation lasts almost three hours. To save Flocke's life, we have to resign ourselves to her never having pups again. Without our fast action to save her, she would have died within hours from blood poisoning.

After the intervention, we bring Flocke, still numb, to the game park's quarantine station to wake up. We shut her in an empty horse stall. Early the next morning, we join her again to see how she's doing. She greets us amiably as if nothing has happened, but we want to keep her quarantined until midday anyway. An hour later, Flocke suddenly runs free through the game park's public parking lot. Nobody can explain how she managed to get out of the stall. She must have watched us close the door and opened it the same way.

I put the escape artist on a leash and decide to bring her to the wolf enclosure instead of back to the stall. Flocke is in a great hurry; I can hardly keep up with her. She wants to return to her pack, and though her fresh wound must still hurt, she is unstoppable. As we reach the enclosure, Chinook and Nanuk rejoice wildly, and Flocke can hardly wait until I open the door of the enclosure. I take off her collar and let her in. To my surprise, she runs purposefully past both wolves without paying any attention to them. Her only interest now is the hole she dug for her pups. She crawls in and examines everything very carefully. With great concentration, she sniffs not only the inside of the den, but also the mountain of sand that we dug out and piled up yesterday. Only after she doesn't find any traces of pups does she shake the sand off her coat and run calmly to Chinook and Nanuk to finally greet them.

Now it is clear to me why Flocke escaped from the stall and strove to get to the enclosure so fast. She was convinced that her newborn pups were waiting for her in the den. Her powerful maternal feelings overcame her pain and strengthened her.

It would have been a great experience for me to see the little wolves grow up. I hoped to take part in the family life of the pack, follow and observe the first steps of the pups, and see them crawl out of the den the first time to explore their environment and get to know the other pack members. I would have liked to know how much of their trust I could gain despite their being raised naturally by their mother, and how much the pups would have accepted me as a human. For me, many questions remain unanswered, but the important thing is that we could save Flocke in time. She will never be able to have her own pups, but I will get another wolf pup in the near future and integrate it into the existing pack so that Flocke, despite her loss, can fulfill her maternal feelings.

Wolf Country: Wolf Distribution Yesterday and Today

From Lord of the Wilderness to Endangered Species

■ My Dream: The Wolves Visit

I dream that I am with my wolves alone somewhere in the wilderness, very far away. They are allowed to run free all day without knowing a fence or a collar, without the danger of meeting another person or having to cross a street. I hear them howling in the darkness. Maybe they're signaling the departure of a hunting trip; maybe they only want to say "We belong together!" or "Hello, here we are, do you hear us?" And I hear them. The cliffs and mountains multiply their howls many times. The echoes fill the air and make it almost impossible to determine exactly where the wolves are. But despite the distance, I can recognize each voice. My heart warms to know that they are all there and doing well. Tomorrow they will surely drop by again. They come silently; only the tracks in the snow reveal them. Then they scratch impatiently on the door of my log cabin until I come out. Together, we run out and scrap in the snow. After a while, all of them are ready to go again—the wilderness calls. With a powerful shake, they rid the last bits of snow from their thick coats, look me over one last time, and trot back to freedom across the white expanse. I stay where I am and enjoy the view, captivated by their fascinating sleekness and the rhythm of their movements until they disappear beyond the horizon.

I often dream this, even though I know that my dream for my wolves will never be realized. I ask myself, where can wolves live as they do in my dream?

Opposite: The European gray wolf is one of the shyest subspecies of the wolf family.

■ Territorial Range

Two hundred years ago, wolves were at home over nearly the entire earth. Now they inhabit only about 10 percent of their original territorial range. Wolves once populated the northern hemisphere from the Arctic to the deserts and even into the tropics, from the lowlands to the high mountains. Today they live in the last wild regions of our earth but also in immediate proximity to humans. Wolves can cope everywhere as hunters of large game or as garbage exploiters, as loners as well as in large packs. For food they rely primarily on mammals from mice to elk, but also insects, berries, and other fruits. In coastal regions, wolves

obtain most of their food from the ocean. Their menu includes fish, mussels, and barnacles.

Influenced by their varied living conditions, numerous wolf subspecies have developed, which can be distinguished by teeth, eye color, coat color, body size, and bone structure. There are roughly a dozen wolf subspecies. Their colors span the range from white to gray to brown to black. The biggest wolves, weighing up to 175 pounds, live in the earth's cold regions. There, all animals are somewhat bigger than their species' members in other places. A body with a large volume can store warmth longer; this protection against cooling is important for survival in northern areas. In hot regions, on the other hand, you find smaller wolves weighing around forty pounds. All of these wolves, whether white or black, small or large, belong to the genus of the gray wolf.

■ Of Wolves and Humans: Some Evolutionary History

At the end of the Ice Age, humans and wolves were the only hunters of large game on the tundra. The great ecological and social similarities between these two species presumably led to a close and long-lasting relationship. Whether humans approached wolves or wolves approached humans can no longer be clearly determined. At any rate, a long and successful connection began. This connection was the beginning of the origin of dogs, which have long since outdistanced the distribution of their progenitor.

In the legends of the Native Americans and Inuit, there is a very distinct image of wolves that displays an exact knowledge of their habits and a deep ecological understanding. The wolf is a symbol of creation and ethnic identity. The natives of North America call the wolf "Brother." In the language of the Sioux, wolves are even labeled *Tashuunka waken*, "Holy Brother." These animals are seen as wise teachers of humanity. The natives of Canada's west coast also express reverence and wonder toward wolves; they immortalize them on their totem poles and cliff drawings. Native Americans and wolves share the same fate; both were mercilessly persecuted almost to extinction.

Over the course of evolutionary history, humans have distanced themselves further and further from animal behavior. They have abandoned their natural lifestyle while wild wolves have retained their original nature. The consequences of the development of humans from hunters and gatherers to farmers and shepherds are fatal to wolves. Wolves not only become people's worst enemy but also compete with hunters and dogs. Through agriculture and animal husbandry, humans remove themselves from natural cycles; they demand more and more land for themselves and their livestock and drive away the wild. In pastures and paddocks, they keep their living "meat locker": pigs, cows, goats, and sheep. Since wolves cannot distinguish between wild and domesticated animals, they occasionally attack livestock. So they often threaten the existence of livestock owners.

As human settlements expand, animal husbandry intensifies, and forests are sacrificed for clearings, the more harsh and frequent the conflicts between humans and wolves become. Added to this tension is the trend of hunting for sport, a leisure-time activity for which people tolerate no animal competition. Human hatred of wolves grows. They come to symbolize animals whose only purpose is to threaten and harm people.

In the eighth century, Charlemagne undertook a decisive campaign to exterminate the wolf. His hunters battled wolves with steel-jaw traps, pits, hooks, nets, and poison. For organized wolf hunts, special dog

Opposite above: Timber wolves are born with a black coat that becomes gray with age.

Opposite below: Though all wolves belong to the gray wolf family, their appearance varies greatly.

55

breeds such as the Irish wolfhound were developed. In the fourteenth century, Charles VI revised the wolf hunt. He eliminated the wolf hunters, legally obligated farmers to destroy wolves, and offered a reward for every animal killed. In some places today, there are still memorials for hunters who chased down the last wolf in their region in the middle of the nineteenth century.

The superstition that the wolf is an embodiment of coming disaster has its origin in the Middle Ages. The wolf was already a symbol of evil in the Old Testament. Fear of the unpredictable and uncontrollable was well established in pictures of witches, devils, and werewolves, in which the character of the bloodthirsty wolf was projected over and over. Wolves' howling was taken as a sign that the "Beast" had made a pact with the devil. These images of wolves say more about people of the past, their fears and concerns, than about wolves themselves.

■ Legends, Myths, Fairy Tales

Almost no other animal has so excited the imagination of people and played such a large role in human cultural history as the wolf. Wolves

Above: The Teutonic peoples revered the wolf as the companion of their supreme god, Odin. In the Christian tradition, the wolf became a symbol of evil.

Opposite left: Since the great wolf hunts, a wolf at play is a rare sight. Wolves only play when they can feel completely secure.

Opposite right: Persecuted by humans, wolves seek refuge more and more frequently in dense forests.

appear as characters in many legends, myths, and fairy tales. Not only the dark side of humans has been projected on wolves.

In the mythology of the Teutonic peoples, two wolves—Geri and Freki—accompany the supreme war god, Odin, and protect him from all dangers. According to Odin, when a wolf howls it is a good omen for the outcome of a battle. But with evil Fenrir—a violent demon in the form of a wolf—comes the downfall of Odin and the whole world. In North Germanic mythology, two wolves named Hati and Scalli chase the moon and the sun across the sky, and in another legend the old Germanic goddess Hyndla rides on a wolf. A Slavic legend tells of a forest spirit named Borowiec who protects his hares, deer, and stags with the help of wolves. He uses them as guard dogs and is called "Lord of the Wolves."

Similarly, the wolf plays an important role in the mythology of the Greeks and Romans. In their myths, the wolf is a protector of humans. According to legend, ancient Rome was founded by Romulus and Remus, who owe their lives to the female wolf, Lupa. Aphrodite, the Greek goddess of love, often appears accompanied by a wolf. Lykaon, King of Arcadia, was transformed into a wolf as he tried to sacrifice his son Arkas to Zeus.

Finally, the Mongolian ruler Genghis Khan was, according to *The Secret History of the Mongols*, supposedly descended from the mythical wolf Bört-a-Tschao.

Where wolves hunt, the forest stays healthy.

Today, human concepts of wolves are still characterized by dramatic opposites. The wolf is either the killer beast, or its image is distorted by an almost supernatural mythos. Neither speaks to reality.

For most people, wolves are mysterious but also potentially dangerous—untamable and uncontrollable. So they represent the opposite of civilization on our too-crowded planet. The more the highways crisscross the land, the more the meadows disappear under subdivisions and asphalt, and the bigger the garbage dumps get, the more the human desire for lost nature grows. In search of something to balance our overtechnological and consumeristic world, people associate the wolf with its original qualities, such as freedom and independence. The wolf has therefore become a symbol of freedom and adventure in the earth's last wilderness. This fascination with the wolf has resulted in a growing interest in the animal, and more and more people oppose the wolf's extermination.

Projects to Protect Wolves

Until the 1970s, wolves were ruthlessly persecuted in Europe and survived only in the inaccessible canyons and mountains of Abruzzo in Italy, the Carpathian Mountains in Romania, and the Cantabrian mountains of Spain. A number of projects to protect European wolves have been underway for about thirty years. In most European Union countries, wolves are strictly protected. The use of poison bait is prohibited in almost all European countries; and Slovakia and Romania no longer allow wolf hunting, at least while pups are being reared.

People's fear and hatred have been somewhat transformed, and in some countries—as in a few areas of North America—wolves have even become tourist attractions.

■ Yellowstone Park

The best-known place to see wolves is probably Yellowstone National Park, the oldest in the United States, in northwest Wyoming and the borderlands of Montana.

The last wolf was killed there eighty years ago under the auspices of an official extermination program. Almost too late, people recognized what a large role wolves play in maintaining ecological balance. They are the last link at the top of the food chain, so they are an important part of a healthy community of life. Wolves prefer to hunt old, weak, or sick animals that make easier prey, helping to ensure a healthy population of game. A proverb of the Inuit, who are closely connected to nature, says, "Where the wolf hunts, the caribou herds are healthy." Another proverb is, "Where wolves hunt, the forest stays healthy." Since the young tree seedlings that play an important role in the regeneration of the forest are delicacies for deer and elk, the overpopulation of hoofed mammals can result in great destruction of young plants. By reducing the impact of these animals, such damage can be minimized.

In the 1990s, over thirty gray wolves were brought from Canada to acclimation enclosures in Yellowstone. After being given ten weeks to adjust, they were fitted with radio collars and set free. Since then, they have increased their numbers to almost three hundred. They have taken up hunting the numerous elk, which are deemed responsible for the destruction of grassy areas. The carcasses the wolves leave behind are a welcome food source for other wild animals such as grizzly bears and eagles. The wolves have also put a check on the number of coyotes, which in turn has resulted in an increase in small rodents that serve as food for foxes, hawks, and eagles.

Despite strict protection, the wolves do not live in the park without danger. Cases are piling up where wolves have been mauled by pumas, run over by cars, or killed in the park's hot springs. In addition, it is gradually becoming too crowded in the park for the constantly growing wolf population. There is enough wild country, but the wolf packs need a certain amount of distance from each other. As it is, wolves wander outside the park more and more frequently, looking for new territory. Their greatest enemies live nearby: the livestock ranchers who fear for their herds on the range. The ranchers tried to legally prevent the reintroduction of the wolves, but their action failed in federal court. Now, although wolves are strictly protected, they can be shot when they are caught killing cattle or sheep.

In contrast to the ranchers, the other residents of Yellowstone are pleased about their new neighbors. Since the wolves howl again there, wolf tourists, nature lovers, and photographers have been coming in droves. With binoculars, they can watch the wolves hunting and traveling, which makes this remote national park especially attractive. The souvenir shops do good business as well, selling stuffed animals, picture books, postcards, and T-shirts with wolf motifs.

A friend of mine who recently took part in a wolf trip in Yellowstone told me about her experiences when she returned:

We set out early in the mornings, with temperatures in the teens. As we arrived in the Lamar Valley forty minutes later, the sun came up and we surveyed the backs of the mountains and the broad valley through binoculars. We usually discovered wolves immediately. They belong to the Druid pack, which has its territory here and is forming splinter groups. When they have eaten enough, they choose a good place where they can see everything and take a nap that sometimes lasts hours. Other wolves go hunting. Game is plentiful in the park. We saw enormous herds of elk and bison as well as bighorn sheep and lone elk.

Opposite: In the protection of the park, the wolves can feel secure.

Plenty of prey and few people. Today, the nearly inaccessible and wild Carpathians are the last great refuge for wolves in Europe.

When a hunt begins, you can see it in the behavior of the chosen prey animals long before the wolves themselves come into view. Once I was standing on a hill when I noticed a cow elk looking intently in one direction. After ten minutes, five gray wolves appeared there; at the same time the herd moved and all of the elk disappeared behind the hill. A little while later, we descended the hill to our car to drive on. Suddenly the cow elk, chased by a wolf, ran across the road and jumped in panic into a little stream. Soon a second wolf was on the spot; both wolves tried to snatch the cow, but she kicked at them. After a while, the wolves gave up; in the water, they had no chance against the wildly kicking elk cow. Maybe they felt bothered by us; we were only about two hundred feet away.

A road with many turnouts goes through the valley. You are only allowed to stop at the turnouts, but many visitors pay no attention to this rule. As soon as wolves appear near the road, everyone hits the brakes, and in no time a dozen cars are stopped. Rangers patrol the park, of course, but they can't be everywhere at once. In winter, when we visited the valley, absolute quiet ruled. In summer, on the other hand, it swarms with tourists who come in buses and cars.

I had the feeling, incidentally, that a few sly wolves use the road for

their hunt, chasing the shy elk to it to confuse them more. The panicked animals make easier prey. We saw carcasses near the road again and again. We also saw a wolf try to cross the road to rejoin its pack. When cars immediately gathered, the wolf had to make a long detour, which was quite laborious in two feet of snow.

Nevertheless, the park is a good thing for the wolves. Here they can live protected.

■ The Carpathians

If Europeans would like to experience wolves in the wild, they do not have to travel to the United States. They have the opportunity to watch wild wolves in Romania, one of the poorest and wildest countries of Europe. The hard-to-access Carpathian Mountains are the retreat of Europe's largest number of predators. Here, along with bear and lynx, lives a stable population of over three thousand wolves, about a third of the entire European population.

Within the framework of ecotourism, a research station in the Carpathians organizes international wolf work camps for youth, wolf-watching trips, and so-called howling excursions. Guests often lodge at private inns; this provides the local population with additional income from tourism.

The farmers and shepherds who live in the Carpathians haven't forgotten how to interact with large predators. The Romanian people have never become strangers to the wolf. They consider wolves a permanent part of nature; they know them and accept them, not simply seeing them as the embodiment of evil. Since there have always been wolves in the countryside, sheep have always needed watching. In addition, traditional methods of livestock husbandry have been preserved in Romania. Shepherds maintain smaller flocks of sheep and often use them for milk. During the day, the sheep are under the eye of shepherds and their specially bred sheepdogs. In the evening, the sheep are brought in for milking behind protective fences or stalls, where they are safe from wolves.

The main danger to these wolves is the destruction of their habitat. The steadily growing number of hunters, which has more than doubled

since the fall of communism in 1989, also causes trouble for the wolves. Many hunters shoot as soon as they get a wolf in their sights. If they kill an alpha wolf, the whole pack can disintegrate. Even if the pack doesn't break up, it takes some time before its hierarchy is reestablished. Without leadership, it is difficult for the wolves to kill enough prey; in the meantime, they attack domesticated animals out of necessity. Therefore, people may achieve exactly the opposite of what they intended by killing a wolf. The thoughtless acts of the hunter increase the chances of harm to people.

The Romanian wolves show great ability to adapt. Some leave the forests to search for food in the cities, coming ever closer to people. Romania's Carpathian Large Carnivore Project observes and protects wolves. One wolf, whom the researchers named Timish, reared her pups in the immediate vicinity of the central Romanian city of Brasov. Her nightly prowls regularly brought her right through the city and the nighttime traffic. No one realized she was a wolf, apparently thinking she was a stray dog. Since she was fitted with a radio collar from the internationally supported research project, her daily habits could be followed precisely. The collar eventually stopped working, however, and now unfortunately there is no sign of her.

The goal of the Carpathian Large Carnivore Project is, among other things, to provide an example of how large predators and people can coexist. And the project shows that they can do just that. People should be made aware of the actual amount of damage caused by wolves. For example, only 2 percent of sheep deaths in the Carpathians are due to wolves. That is about three thousand sheep per year, or an average of one sheep per wolf, a comparatively small loss.

Opposite: Wolves are taking back lost territories through their ability to adapt.

Italy and France

Wolves not only venture into the suburbs in Romania but also into those of Italy, where they have discovered garbage dumps as a new food source. They are jokingly called "spaghetti wolves" because they eat left-over noodles at the dumps, among other things: further evidence of the adaptability of the gray wolf species.

The Italian wolf population is constantly growing and expanding its territory. Wolves are spreading along the Apennine mountain chain north toward France and Switzerland.

In France, meanwhile, there is a small wolf population of slightly less than a hundred animals. The Alpine region, where the wolves live today, is well populated with chamois, mouflon, and ibex. In the summer months, hundreds of sheep are herded onto mountain pastures where they are generally unguarded. For a hunting wolf, this is like an invitation to a set table, so conflicts between livestock owners and wolves are unavoidable. Angry sheep owners protest and demand that the government permit the shooting of wolves.

Switzerland

Since some of Switzerland's neighboring countries have unusually high populations of wild wolves, lone wolves from Italy and France have recently wandered repeatedly into the country. The first migrants are mainly young males who rely almost completely on domesticated animals due to their limited hunting experience. Wherever wolves have been exterminated in past centuries, their reappearance causes a great stir and unleashes intense discussions. In light of this, a survey carried out by the World Wildlife Fund in Switzerland produced a surprising result: seventy-seven percent of the more than a thousand Swiss surveyed approved of the wolves' reappearance. It would be especially interesting to know how many of those surveyed were farmers.

Many sheep farmers are outraged by the wolves' return. As in France, livestock owners in the Swiss Alps have no experience with wolves. For economic reasons, the sheep graze there more or less unguarded and are merely checked on once or twice a week. These animals pose yet another problem. Without management, they graze some areas too heavily, which leads to damaged pastures and erosion. With just under half a million sheep in Switzerland, conflicts with wolves are inevitable. Such unguarded animals are easy prey for wolves, and where wolves once have a successful hunt, they return again and again.

◼ Excursus: Hunting Instinct and Domestic Animals

Pursued and panicked sheep trigger a number of hunting instincts in wolves, who often kill more prey than they can eat. This behavior is natural for all predators. A marten in a flock of doves or a fox in a hen-house behaves exactly the same way. In Germany's Krefeld Zoo, cheetahs freed by animal rights activists unleashed a true massacre one night in the neighboring kangaroo enclosure without eating a single animal. Similarly, house cats also do not have to be suffering from hunger to catch a mouse or songbird.

To make this easier to understand, I can fall back on my experiences with my wolves. They know from the time they are young that they are regularly allowed to go walking on the leash in the game park. They also know their animal "neighbors" and almost always remain indifferent to them, regardless of whether we walk past enclosures holding red deer, sheep, or goats. This works perfectly up to a certain point. But if the other animals are scared for some reason, react in panic, and attempt to flee, the hunting instinct of the wolves immediately awakens; the wolves view the nervous animals as suitable prey. In the moment, they're unconcerned with the fact that they ate an entire deer earlier that day and their bellies are so full they can hardly run. It's in their blood to quickly

Wolves hunt their prey together with cleverly devised strategies. Circling their prey is a successful hunting tactic.

recognize and take advantage of a good hunting opportunity, and this is crucial to their survival.

Hunting instinct is perhaps strengthened by their membership in the pack: wolves must always hunt for all of their companions and immediately strike at such an opportunity, since they can never foresee when the next prey will offer itself. Animals with limited possibilities to flee their enclosure probably call forth exactly the same reaction from my gentle wolves as unprotected sheep herds do from wild wolves. The hunting reflex is set off by the prey animals' unnatural behavior. In the wild, you would never see a case of a hunting wolf pack "senselessly" killing twenty deer.

Domestication allows people to hold a large number of animals in the smallest possible space. Through breeding and selection over millennia, people have eliminated shyness in domesticated species. We have bred more trusting and easily manipulated animals and therefore have simultaneously made them more vulnerable to predators. Over time, various methods of protecting the herds were developed but were forgotten with the extermination of wolves. Before the first wolves returned

to almost predator-free Switzerland, a negative attitude about predators had been generated by lynxes gone wild. The consequence is poaching, and most wolves are illegally shot as soon as they appear. Only a few of these cases become well-known. Meanwhile, the damage to domestic animals grows, especially to unguarded sheep in the canton of Wallis, bordering Italy and France.

If the damage to a herder's livestock exceeds a tolerable level, the Swiss government grants a permit to shoot the culpable wolf. But financial compensation from the government does not satisfy the sheep owners. Their losses often entail interruptions in long breeding lines and the ruin of many years' work. The sheep owners are embittered and even suspect environmentalists of secretly reintroducing wolves. Genetic tests show, however, that their problems have to do with the natural immigration of wolves from Italian populations.

The Swiss Department of Environment, Food, and Rural Affairs is preparing proposals and projects to address the concerns of farmers without exterminating the wolf again. By law, the wolf is protected in Switzerland, but as long as there are conflicts between people and wolves, this protection is ineffective. The challenge of the coming years will be to revive old methods of protection and develop new ones. Protection of the herds with sheepdogs and a fence or hut at night is essential. Donkeys—who show amazing bravery when resisting wolves, foxes, or stray dogs—should be used again as well. Of course the problem cannot be solved without the cooperation and initiative of sheep owners and shepherds. Only when human and wolf can live side by side will wolves be protected from persecution. This applies to all people in those areas that are newly experiencing wolves or other large predators.

■ Germany

Germany is another country to which wolves are migrating. One by one, they appear in the states of Mecklenburg-Vorpommern, Brandenburg, and Saxony. They swim across the River Oder between Poland and Germany. Others take a route over the southern Polish border and follow the high ridges of the Carpathians and Sudetes into the Erz Mountains. Early in 2000, a three-legged wolf named Naum near Eisenhüttenstadt on the border with Poland caused headlines. He presumably lost his right rear foot in a trap and then chased a sheepdog. Since his handicap caused fears that he might attack domestic animals, he was captured and put in an enclosure at the Schorfheide Game Park.

The greatest wolf event, though, happened not sixty miles from densely settled Berlin. For the first time in more than 150 years, a wild wolf reared her young in the Muskauer heath, on a 200-square-mile military proving ground. This Lausitzer wolf pack enjoys great sympathy from the majority of the population. Casualties among domestic animals have been low so far and are generously compensated by the state of Saxony. If the wolves attack unprotected livestock or dogs, however, the local residents could lose their enthusiasm and old, nearly forgotten primal fears would be aroused.

Despite the sympathy of the population and strict protection, lone wolves are often mistaken for stray dogs and shot. In the beginning of November 2002, a wild wolf appeared in Lower Saxony for the first time in two centuries. During its journey through the southern part of the district of Göttingen to the edge of the Harz Mountains, it attacked sheep twice but avoided people. After some time, walkers in the woods discovered an animal that they believed was a wild dog with a freshly

Opposite: The wolf is returning to Germany.

killed deer. A hunter called to the scene felt threatened by the growling "sheepdog" and shot the only living wolf in Lower Saxony. An examination of the microchip carried by the dead wolf revealed that she was a wolf named Bärbel who had escaped from a game park in Vogtland six months earlier. This "enclosure wolf" adapted to freedom amazingly fast. She put hundreds of miles behind her on her travels through Vogtland and Bohemia to Lower Saxony, and with two exceptions fed herself exclusively on wild animals. Her tragic death drew grief and anger from her fans. The hunter who shot her even received numerous death threats.

I was also very sad about her death. On the other hand, I was aware, without prejudice, that this wolf could in fact have been dangerous for imprudent people such as wolf lovers or children. Despite all our goodwill toward the wolf, we must not forget that it is a predator and that accidents can happen even with tame or half-tame animals. Bärbel was born in captivity. Although she attempted to avoid contact with people when possible during her journey, her shyness and readiness to flee from people were not as developed as they would be in a wild wolf. The walkers did not disturb her while she was eating, and even the hunter got within a few yards of her. Instead of fleeing, she circled him and attempted to defend her prey, for which she ultimately paid with her life. Wolves are protected by European Union law, and the hunter unknowingly violated the species act that applies to them.

Despite her regrettable death, the escaped wolf Bärbel filled an important role. She made the media aware of her and roused people's interest in wild wolves. Fortunately, a direct, momentous confrontation between her and humans didn't occur. Even the smallest damage could have ruined years of education about wild wolves. The nearly vanquished image of the bloodthirsty beast would have been newly awakened and the enthusiasm of the people for the wolf's return to Germany would have been set back.

Poland

In Germany's neighboring country, Poland, the wolf population is estimated to be about eight hundred animals. More exact counts are difficult

to make. Despite the proximity of people, numerous wolf packs live there, including in the resort area of the Schlesian Beskid Mountains near the border of Slovakia, where the valleys are densely populated and skiers romp down the steep mountain slopes in winter. The wolves apparently do not let themselves be disturbed by them.

Another wolf region is in the forests of western Poland. This 150-square-mile contiguous forest preserve, not an hour's drive from the German-Polish border, offers wolves optimal living conditions. In Poland, wolves were hunted until the middle of the 1990s. They have only been protected year-round since 1998. In 2001, international animal defense funds launched a project to protect the Polish wolves.

■ Scandinavia

The pristine and expansive wild forests of Scandinavia could shelter a sizeable population of wolves. But a majority of the Scandinavian population harbors a generally negative attitude about predators. The reasons for this are reindeer herding in Norway and interest in elk hunting in Sweden.

Wolves are hated, and persecuted through every means. Wolf hunting with snowmobiles is especially effective, and the last wolf in Norway was killed this way in the 1970s. At the beginning of the 1990s, a single pair of wolves that suffered from heavy inbreeding remained in Sweden. According to researchers, every native wolf in Sweden is descended from a single male who immigrated to Sweden from Finland and bred with the female of this pair. This male presumably increased genetic diversity and led to the recovery of the Swedish wolf population. But numbering only about one hundred wolves today, the entire Scandinavian population is still very small. Scientists in Sweden and Norway assume that at least five hundred wolves need to live in Scandinavia to form a secure basis for the future.

Opposite: Long migrations of single young males safeguard the wolf population in all of Scandinavia.

■ Spain

About two thousand wolves still live in Spain. Livestock is plentiful there, especially sheep and goats, some of which are killed by illness or accidents. These carcasses are one of the most important food sources for Spanish wolves. For this reason, sheepherding, among other things, is promoted by the conservation group Euronatur.

An acquaintance who has lived a long time in Spain told me about a neighboring farmer who, while harvesting his grain fields, found whole litters of young wolves on the bare ground many times. Until I heard this, I believed that wolves only had pups in dens. The wolves in this area apparently depend on these enormous fields offering them enough protection. The farmer killed the first pups he found. Later, he took three pups home. They couldn't have been even ten days old, since they were still blind. The farmer's family attempted to rear them. One female survived and has eked out her sad existence since then in a small, dirty kennel in the backyard.

■ Russia

Today, about 40 percent of all wild wolves in the world are found in regions of the former Soviet Union. Living conditions for the animals

in Russia are by no means easy. Wolves are traditionally regarded as a dangerous enemy of livestock there; they are hunted year-round with all methods, including such unsportsmanlike ones as hunting from airplanes and using snares or poison, which are forbidden for use on other wild animals.

Anyone searching for the adventure of a wolf hunt can book such a trip very easily on the Internet. Numerous Web sites advertise wolf hunts in areas with an "exploding wolf population" and say such things as "Population control shootings are necessary to avoid sacrificing deer." The most recent research of Russian wolf experts reveals, however, that the officially cited high wolf numbers are not correct, and that in fact the Russian wolf population is sharply declining. Nevertheless, wolf shoots continue to be promoted and sold to foreign-currency-toting trophy hunters and wealthy natives from the city. Professional hunters bring guests to specially arranged areas with viewing blinds, or they organize "turkey shoots" with helicopters, all-terrain vehicles, or snowmobiles. Despite all of these methods, hunting shy wolves is difficult, and the organizers only earn their money when a wolf is actually shot. For this reason, they often buy wolf pups and rear them to later drive them in front of the clueless hunters.

A few members of a biological station in the Tver region between Moscow and St. Petersburg are helping protect and preserve wolves in that area, which has the greatest wolf concentration in European Russia. With the help of volunteers and students, experiments are being conducted there to make a reliable count of the wild wolf population. Simple methods of protecting herds and deterring wolves are also being developed. In Russia, dogs are only rarely used to protect herds, and wolves far too often kill the few dogs that are employed. Therefore, other ways to protect livestock are needed. Such simple things as colorful fabrics, rustling cellophane, and glistening strips of aluminum foil attached to paddock fences have proven effective. In addition, some sheep carry bells on their throats. These kinds of protection exploit wolves' natural caution and shyness and raise hopes that the eternal conflict between livestock farmers and wolves may be somewhat alleviated. But as long as the government allows the use of poison lures for "population control" and pays out bounties for dead wolves, it will be almost impossible to change Russians' minds about wolves.

Not long ago, I had the opportunity to talk with a young gamekeeper from Kirghizstan in Central Asia. He sometimes travels for months at a time in a remote mountainous region, a wilderness with permanent snow and countless glaciers. His job is to protect the endangered snow leopard that lives there from poachers and illegal furriers. Over a cozy cup of tea, he told me about the leopards and other animals of this region. Along with ibexes, Siberian deer, bears, and snow leopards, wolves still live there, and this interested me the most, of course. He reported that he often finds their tracks in the snow and has often observed them running past his log cabin base camp.

I got out my photo album of innumerable wolf pictures. We paged through it, with me commenting on the images and him listening intently. Since his connection with nature and true wilderness were so unfamiliar to me, and I was touched by his enthusiasm for wolves, I suggested that we visit my wolves in the enclosure. To my surprise, instead of the approval I expected, he adamantly refused. In Russia, hatred for wolves is deeply rooted. They are loathed not only by livestock owners and farmers but also by the general population. Even among zoologists, biologists, and people connected to nature, no good relationship with wolves can be found. This does not just have to do with "Little Red Riding Hood syndrome," by the way, which we often use to try to explain hatred of wolves in Europe. From time immemorial, the wolf has been a competitor for food in the poor parts of Russia as it poaches sparse herds of livestock.

Nevertheless, in old Russian fairy tales the wolf is not the embodiment of evil, but rather a hero and helper. There is the story of a lonely hunter, for example, who frees a wolf from a trap and saves its life. In gratitude, the wolf leads him to an orchard

The wolf—not just the embodiment of evil but also a helper in Russian myths and fairy tales.

in a secret place, where an old apple tree bears very special fruit; if you eat one of these apples, you remain eternally young. The hunter picks an apple and eats it but continues to feel unhappy and is even lonelier than before. The wolf says he can help the hunter with this, too. He takes the hunter on his back and carries him through high mountains and deep forests until he finally reaches his destination. He brings the hunter to a beautiful woman. They fall in love, marry, and are happy. The wolf then disappears into the wilderness. However, reality for wolves in today's Russia is different from this old fairy tale, which is still read aloud to children. It will take a while before people recognize the wolf's significance there, set aside their prejudices, and finally understand that protecting wolves means taking care of all other animal species and maintaining an intact environment.

■ My Dream: Singing and Listening

Deep in the night, my dream comes again, the dream of free and carefree wolves trotting through the landscape. I can only make out their dark silhouettes backlit by the full moon. They run and run, without turning around, until they reach a small rise on the horizon. There they stay, stepping from one foot onto the other in excitement, howling, wagging their tails, and dancing around each other until one of them raises its snout toward the sky and begins singing the first verse of the wolf song. In no time, they all howl together. Despite my distance, I can see their hot breath in the frosty air.

The somewhat eerie though simultaneously melodic and indescribably beautiful song echoes through the night; it tells of endless hunting parties, immeasurable distances, and the fulfillment of their desire to be free. The different voices and tones of the individual wolves create the impression of a much bigger wolf pack. It is an overwhelming spectacle. After a while, the song is over. The wolves remain motionless and look out from the rise over the open plain. Each of them looks in a different direction, pricks up its ears, and waits to see if a reply comes out of the stillness. But this time, too, their call remains unheard. They do not give up, however. Every night they return here, calling and waiting.

Whether the wolves in my dream receive an answer from their brothers and sisters in reality rests in the hands of humans.

What Can Wolves Mean to People?

Wolves and Death

I had so much planned for today, but then the telephone rings. A woman calls from Bremen, and little by little I gather that she has a terminal illness. She tells me the story of her advanced leukemia, about the suffering that she already has behind her and what is yet to come, and about her last and greatest wish: her dream is to meet wolves, get to know them, and be allowed to touch them. The woman's fate touches me more and more, and she shares with me that in ten days she will undergo a treatment that will determine whether she lives or dies. Since she knows that her chances are not good, she would definitely like to realize her dream before her stay in the hospital. I listen quietly to her thoughts about visiting. She is not sure if she will find enough energy to make it through her longed-for encounter with the wolves. Sometimes she feels better; sometimes she is very weak. A visit will depend on how she feels on a given day. I propose that she call me as soon as she feels able to make the trip.

After the conversation, I stay by the phone, feeling emotional. Everything I had planned for the day is forgotten. I attempt to understand the terminally ill woman, to put myself in her thoughts, her situation. Why is it her last wish to meet wolves? If I were in her situation, I presume I would gladly embrace my wolves one more time and say farewell—but why would she, who has never had any special relationship with wolves before her illness, want to do so? How does the desire to meet a wolf come to this woman who is so close to death?

■ The Wolf as Companion for the Soul

Wolves and death are bound by a deeply mystical relationship. In European history, the wolf always appears as a companion to those crossing into the other world. Herecura, the goddess of death who stands at the threshold to the underworld, has the protection of the wolf on her side. Hekate, who separates the living from those who must go to the underworld, guards the threshold with her wolf. According to Germanic mythology, the soul rides on a female wolf. The wolf also belongs to the creatures of the game hunt, whereby the souls of the dead travel through

Opposite: Wolves and death are bound by a deeply mystical relationship.

the air. In Egypt, Anubis, the god of the dead and companion of the soul, accompanies the dead on their way to the other world. He takes part in the ceremony of opening the mouth, supervises the process of embalming and mummification, protects the mummy, and places the heart on the scales of justice during the judging of the dead. The cult of Anubis was especially revered in Lykopolis, the so-called wolf city.

What all of these myths have in common is that, according to the ancient understanding of the soul, wolves accompany the dead to the other world and assist them with their journey. They can appear as guides on this path, guardians of the gate, and helpers with the rites of passage. With their white color, tundra wolves symbolize the spirit world, the invisible reality. This is the world that shamans travel in and that humans enter when they must die.

Opposite: With their white color, tundra wolves symbolize the spirit world.

The conversation with the woman touches me deeply. It is not the first time I try to fulfill such a wish for an incurably ill person. Recently, a man called me from Holland. He told me about his best friend, a woman suffering from cancer. I grasped the reason for his call only when he reported that her last wish was to experience being close to a wolf. It was difficult for me to agree to this wish, since foot-and-mouth disease had just broken out, and the first cases had appeared in Holland. Foot-and-mouth, feared and highly contagious, is a nightmare for every owner of a hoofed mammal, since it must be battled with radical methods. If one animal gets sick, then all the animals in the whole area must be killed to stop its spread. For this reason alone, I hesitated. I work in a game park, and if our animals were infected in this way, I would reproach myself for the rest of my life. I suggested that he wait a couple of weeks until the disease was under control in Holland. But he persisted. Since his friend didn't have much longer to live and couldn't wait, the trip had to be taken soon, as long as she had enough energy. He prodded and pleaded with me. Despite my reservations, we ultimately arranged a meeting for the following week.

I thought about the meeting the entire week. How would we do it? The woman was seriously ill. Would she manage to keep up with us and the wolves on a walk? And how would the wolves react to a deathly

ill person? Wolves often have no mercy for the weak and even kill pack members whose weakness hinders the pack. During our walks, everyone who goes along is quickly taken into the pack. How would the wolves react to such a weak person?

■ Encounter

Though it has rained the whole week, on the day we meet in the parking lot of the game park, the sun is shining. The woman is the last one to get out of the car. Her face is pale, but her eyes sparkle with great expectation. We greet each other briefly, and without losing any more time, we go to the wolves. They notice us immediately, and from a distance we can already see all three jumping impatiently along the fence. We put them on leashes and head out. Or better said, we gallop away. Happy to be walking, the wolves yank on their leashes and set the tempo for the first few hundred yards. Gradually the distance between us and the woman and her companion grows. After the wolves have run out their initial surplus of energy, though, they stop once in a while to sniff in the grass. So the two catch up to us again.

We go on silently together. I know that the woman is close to dying, and I am not sure how to act. To show sympathy would be inappropriate. So I try to act very normal, and to interrupt the silence I explain various things about the wolves. While she is listening to me, I notice her fleeting attempt to pet Chinook

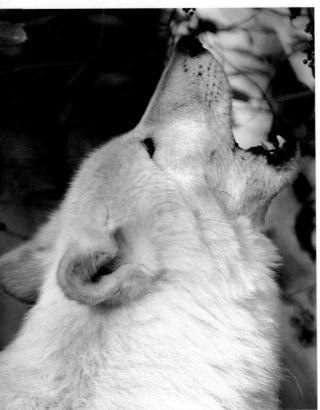

The deeply touching encounter with Chinook makes time seem to stand still for everyone.

on the head as he walks right next to me. When we approach a clearing in the forest I give her Chinook's leash; now she can lead the wolf herself. The two stop at once. Chinook lifts his head toward her, and she bends over toward him. I hear her whisper something in his ear. Suddenly she seems to have forgotten everything around her. No past or future exist for her; in these minutes there is only the present. Sensitive Chinook feels this. He carefully sniffs her face and licks her tenderly. The woman smiles happily, embraces the wolf around the neck, and pulls him against her. Normally, wolves do not like to be hugged and squeezed. This makes them feel crowded and pestered. But instead of trying to get away from the embrace, Chinook stays put and even cuddles with her. I take a couple of pictures of the two. This encounter deeply impresses me; time stands still for me, too. The ringing of a cell phone brings us back to reality. The woman's ten-year-old son is calling: "Mama, are you doing well?" She doesn't hear the question and just says, "Guess where I am right now! Guess who I petted! Guess who just kissed me . . . !" Although her voice is full of enthusiasm, she speaks very quietly; she is already very tired.

Soon we stand in front of the wolf enclosure again. Two hours have flown by. Overwhelmed by her experiences, the woman just wants to go home now. I promise to send her pictures, and the two get on their way back to Holland.

A week later, the friend of my Dutch visitor calls once again to ask about the photographs, which I have just picked up that day, and begs me to send them as fast as possible. He reports that his friend is doing very badly. On her own initiative, she has let herself out of the hospital to go

Long after departure from the enclosure, the farewell song of the wolf can be heard.

home, because she knows the end is near and she would like to be with her family for her last days. I can hardly believe it; she was just here with the wolves and me. And she told me that she had three whole months more to live. I scan the photos immediately and send them via e-mail.

Only a few days later the man reaches me on the phone again. He tells me that his friend died the previous night and adds: "Thanks again for the pictures. I printed them out and brought them to her right away. They made her very happy. Since she was already too weak to even hold the photos, she asked me to attach them to the ceiling above her bed. That way she could always look at them. The pictures of the white wolves accompanied her into death."

Although I only saw the woman once and knew her fleetingly, I am very sad to hear about her death. I still see her beaming happily while embracing Chinook. I hear how she whispers in his ear and shortly thereafter reports the experience to her little son. Along with my sadness, I simultaneously feel satisfaction and gratitude: we were allowed to fulfill this woman's last wish, which was so important to her in the time of her parting from life.

■ Energy Animal

The story of this encounter is not only very moving for me on a personal level. Beyond that, it shows the deep and hidden meaning that the wolf can have for people. For this deathly ill woman, the wolf became her energy animal and inner companion for the path ahead. The life-giving, unbridled, and yet tender wolf-being joins a person's own energy as death approaches. The experience of untamed nature leads people back to their own origin. In this way, the wolf accompanies the human soul on its final path.

The woman bound herself to this old tradition spontaneously and perhaps unconsciously when she searched for and entered a relationship with the white wolves at the end of her life. By having the pictures of the wolves she had been with put on the ceiling above her bed during the last days of her life, she remained in contact with her soul's companion. She entrusted her soul to the white wolf, who protected her and led her on her great crossing.

The woman from Bremen, whom I introduced at the beginning of this chapter, may have expected something similar. An encounter with a wolf had also become incredibly important to her before her death. She, too, intuitively sensed the connection between the white wolf and the crossing into the other world. Unfortunately, I could not fulfill her last wish. Though we had arranged a meeting, she had to cancel at the last minute because she was not physically able to make the trip to the wolves and me.

Opposite: In European history, wolves appear again and again as companions for the crossing into the other world.

84

Struggle for Chinook's Survival

It is the beginning of April. After a long winter and an unfriendly spring, it is finally getting warmer. Fog, rain, wind, and cold, which were part of the daily routine, are forgotten. Nature awakens. The fresh green foliage, clear blue sky, and sunshine are like a balm for the soul after the gray days. Nevertheless, we have no time to enjoy the spring. The breeding season among our raptors is in full swing. The incubators are filled with eggs, and the first hatched and always-hungry baby birds demand our attention almost around the clock. As happens every spring, there is less time for the wolves than usual. I drive with my husband to the wolf enclosure during our lunch break. We have about an hour to see to the wolves: to feed them, clean their enclosure, and distribute affection.

■ Good-bye

The wolves recognize our vehicle from far away, and when we arrive they stand impatiently at the gate to greet us wildly. Today is a day like every other, but immediately we notice that the wolves' greeting delegation is incomplete. Chinook is missing. This is very unusual. I look into the enclosure and discover him lying motionless behind a tree trunk. What is going on? I jump out of the vehicle with my husband behind me. That Chinook doesn't even respond to the loud sounds of the car doors slamming unsettles me even more. He lifts his head only when I open the gate and stands up very ponderously.

His movements have not been as lithe as the younger wolves' for a long time. Since he acquired age-induced osteoporosis a couple of years ago, he no longer likes to jump high or over obstacles, and he requires a certain amount of time during our walks together to warm up and get his joints moving again. Despite all of this, he can still keep up with the rest of the pack.

Chinook shakes the sand out of his coat and runs up to us. My heart skips a beat. I bend over to him and embrace him: "Hello, my boy! What's wrong with you? Do you know that you gave me a great scare?" Chinook snuggles up very close to me. He has always been cuddly, but

Good-bye nears.

today I sense that he is somehow different. I sit down on a tree stump, and the old wolf follows me and gently yet very firmly presses his head onto my lap.

As a rule, as soon as I sit down I am besieged by all the wolves at once. They jump up on me and lick my face to greet me. Each one wants to be the first. Not today, however. Even the impetuous and somewhat jealous Nanuk stands next to Flocke and quietly watches me tickle Chinook between the ears and pet his head. After a while, Chinook turns around and goes to my husband. As with me, he presses his forehead firmly against Lothar's legs. Lothar looks at me and says, very seriously, "I think Chinook would like to say good-bye to us." I, too, notice that today not only Chinook but the other wolves as well behave very oddly and seem depressed and serious. But I can find no direct explanation for this.

We spend a while with the wolves and then drive away. The second raptor presentation begins shortly; the audience is already waiting. Before it starts, we call the veterinarian and make an appointment for after the presentation. An hour later, we all meet in the wolf enclosure. Once again, only Nanuk and Flocke greet us. Chinook can't stand up. There is a small wooden hut in the enclosure. The wolves rarely use it, only when it rains for days. It is here that we discover Chinook. He is lying on his side, his eyes closed. I crawl to him and lift his head up with both hands. He seems apathetic, lifeless; he doesn't even open his eyes. I whisper: "Don't be stupid, my boy, don't give up."

Whimpering, Flocke and Nanuk push themselves through the narrow entrance to the hut. Despite his closed eyes, Chinook notices them immediately and growls at them. He wants them to leave him alone. Nevertheless, Flocke wriggles past me like an eel, bends over Chinook and nudges him with her nose, yowling. At first, Chinook doesn't react. Flocke doesn't give up, though, and carefully chews the coat on his neck with her front teeth. In this way, she gets him to stand up. Her well-meaning care is a burden for him, however. Growling, he avoids her gestures of encouragement as much as he still can. You often read that a weak or sick wolf will be cast out or even killed by its own pack members, but the exact opposite is apparent here. Only now do I notice that Chinook's entire neck is damp. Flocke and Nanuk must have been trying unsuccessfully to get Chinook back on his feet against his will for some time.

We lure Flocke out of the hut and block the entrance with a solid steel grate. This is the only way the two veterinarians who have arrived in the

meantime can examine Chinook without being disturbed. At first glance, the wolf doesn't look sick at all. His coat shines, his eyes are clear, and he doesn't appear to be in pain. The veterinarians determine, however, that his heart is beating irregularly; his relatively low body temperature unsettles them, as well. They take blood for further tests and give him medications to build his strength.

■ Illness, Old Age, and Death

The following days are like a nightmare as we continually alternate between hope and powerlessness, doubt and disappointment. At first, I want to leave Chinook in the enclosure, since I fear that separation from his pack would further strain the weakened wolf. But as his body temperature drops threateningly hour by hour, I have to act fast. Since the nights are still very cold at this time of year, I decide to take the exhausted Chinook home with me to provide him with enough warmth. I push aside the living room furniture and lay him on the floor next to the radiator. I spend the night beside him. I hear how he pants. With one hand, I hold a bowl of water in front of his mouth; with the other, I support his head so he can drink. As soon as he quenches his thirst, however, he spits everything up, and as soon as he empties his stomach he greedily demands water again. He tries to stand up and tips the water bowl over. His diarrhea does not improve the situation, either. I can't think of sleeping. But I'm eventually able to stabilize his body temperature in the warm house.

The next morning I prepare a stall for Chinook in the quarantine station of the game park. I make the space smaller by stacking straw bales along the walls, to make sure he stays directly under the heat lamp. The veterinarians are constant visitors, but his condition doesn't improve. On the contrary, he gets weaker and weaker. He refuses all nourishment, and even the daily injections of medications and electrolytes are no longer enough to sustain him. It's obvious that he doesn't struggle; he gives up. But I don't want to leave any option untried, and I fax all laboratory results to numerous veterinarians in the hope that one of them can provide a new, possibly helpful diagnosis—indeed that maybe a miracle

Dejected mood in the pack. The missing wolf leaves a palpable absence.

will happen. But the same answer comes from everyone: the results are consistent with the age of the animal. Negative.

The struggle for Chinook's survival has lasted for almost a week now. This afternoon he is doing especially badly. He breathes very heavily and for several hours he hasn't even been able to drink anything. I moisten his dry nose and mouth with a wet washcloth. Filled with doubt, I call the veterinarian, but when he arrives, he doesn't know what else to do either. "The only thing that would still make sense," he says, "is to give Chinook an infusion directly into his bloodstream to prevent him from dehydrating. Unfortunately, I don't have enough time for that today because of an important appointment." I immediately tell him that I'm prepared to finish the procedure myself, if that is possible. He agrees.

He fastens two infusion bottles containing the lifesaving fluid to the wall of the stall with a cord, shaves one of Chinook's front legs, and puts a hypodermic needle in a vein. Then he puts a stopper in my hand and gives me further instructions: "You have to be careful that Chinook doesn't move anymore; if he does, the needle could come out. The fluid should only drip in the bloodstream one drop per second; here's where you can adjust it," he says and shows me the regulator on the plastic tube. "When the serum runs out, you carefully pull the tube out and close the

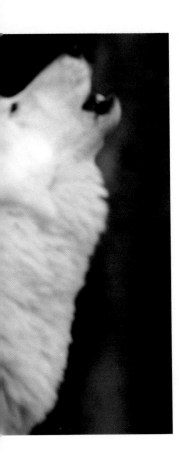

syringe with this stopper. It must sit exactly right. If there's a leaky spot, the animal could bleed to death in a couple of hours." I listen intently and hope I can follow all of his instructions correctly. I lie down next to Chinook to hold his paw completely still and try to find a position I can hold for a couple of hours. The veterinarian leaves; he's in a hurry. I hear him close the car door, start the car, and drive off. The sounds of the motor fade away.

We are alone. Everything is quiet. Chinook lies very still, not resisting anything I do. I've laid my head on his shoulder, and my eyes follow every drop of the infusion. Plop, plop, plop; I find myself counting them: 97, 98, 99 . . . electrolytes and medicine drip into his veins every second, just as they should.

I sense Chinook's muscles relaxing; his breath falters. This scares me. What time is it, anyway? I try to read my watch in the muted light. Ten-thirty. The medication has been dripping into Chinook's weak body for over two hours. Despite the heat lamp, it's getting quite cool. I snuggle close against my wolf and pull a blanket over us. We warm each other. Time appears to stand still. Plop, plop, plop, the fluid quietly drips.

Again and again, from the way Chinook stretches his leg out and bends his back, I sense his muscles cramping. It's just after midnight. Soon we'll have finished. One bottle of medicine is empty, and there isn't much left in the second. Nevertheless, Chinook is doing worse. He begins to pant with his mouth wide open; his heart races. I let go of his leg. I quickly remove the plastic tube and close the open syringe with the stopper. The tube is barely removed when Chinook twitches violently and tries desperately to stand up. I push him to the floor with my shoulder. I have to secure the needle as fast as possible, but I can't. Chinook won't hold still; his reactions get more and more intense. I can't hold him down anymore. His eyes are wide open; his gaze is empty. He doesn't react to my calls; he appears not to perceive me at all. Blood squirts through the open syringe and colors his white coat red. I manage to take out the needle and then jump out of the stall to get a bandage from my car.

I return a few seconds later and can only watch powerlessly as the fit reaches its climax. Chinook's whole body twitches and shivers; his cramped, open mouth foams. Sticky with his own spit, blood, urine, and excrement, he staggers confusedly from wall to wall and snaps at everything in his way. He has totally lost control of himself. He bites down so hard that his gums bleed in several places. Suddenly, he stands, wobbling in one spot, then collapses, totally exhausted. All of this takes only a few minutes, but to me it seems like an eternity.

I quietly encourage Chinook. He opens his eyes and looks at me. I notice that his awareness is gradually returning. I bandage his leg and clean his coat with straw. Then I put his exhausted body forward a little, so that he's right under the heat lamp. While I'm doing this, Chinook lifts his head laboriously and briefly licks my hand. Then he lies down again; he is dead tired. I pet him and think about the misery he's just gone through. I begin to doubt whether we have the right to preserve this wolf's life at any price. Without the medications, his heart probably would have stopped beating long ago.

First thing the next morning I call the veterinarian to tell him what happened. "It was an epileptic seizure," he says. "Epilepsy is a disease of the central nervous system. Chinook's diseased heart and weakened lungs can't manage to provide his brain with enough oxygen anymore." Then he makes an appointment for me to bring Chinook for an X ray again at midday. The veterinary clinic is very close by, not ten minutes away by car. Nevertheless, Chinook has a second seizure on the way, and as we arrive at the waiting room, he's unconscious. Examinations and X rays follow and finally the veterinarian stands in front of us with the results. His facial expression is serious, and even before he says anything I know that we have lost this battle. Further measures would be senseless. The veterinarian takes out a syringe and relieves the unconscious Chinook.

I drive home and with the feeling that my wolf is present all around me. My clothes smell like him; his hair is everywhere. I change my clothes, and everything that I wore while handling him goes into the washing machine.

Despite my sadness, I feel relief: at last Chinook has no more pain!

This afternoon, everything must go on as usual, as if nothing has happened. First, the raptor presentation, then taking care of the birds,

Opposite: For a long time, people denied that animals have feelings. The wolves' mourning for Chinook is clearly apparent, however.

checking incubation machines, and preparing food for the baby birds. In the evening, I drive to the park, as always, to feed the young birds. When all of the hungry beaks are finally satisfied, it occurs to me that I have completely neglected my other wolves over the last week. During the time I spent with Chinook, Lothar took care of Flocke and Nanuk.

■ Wolf Mourning

It's still light out, and I spontaneously decide to drive to the wolf enclosure.

"A meager pack!" I think as I see the two remaining wolves from a distance. It'll take some time for me to get accustomed to this sight. I get out of the car and run silently to the enclosure. Flocke and Nanuk can hardly wait to greet me and whimper loudly with happiness. They jump up excitedly on the gate, and as I go to open it, they both greet me by licking my hand through the bars of the fence. Then they stop suddenly in their excitement, clinging to the fence, and stick their noses through to sniff my hand more precisely. Instinctively, I jerk back. But it's too late; they've noticed. From the fine traces of scent that still linger on my skin since midday, they can read and incorporate the sad message lightning fast. Chinook is dead.

With raised ears, they both look me in the eyes as if searching for an explanation. Then they slowly turn and walk side by side to the

Flocke and Nanuk do not grasp the finality of death.

old, horizontal oak trunk in the middle of the enclosure. With ease, they jump up on the trunk and begin howling, muzzle to muzzle. No, it isn't howling, it sounds much more like a farewell song, and only the three of us know whom it is for. They howl for a long time; it almost seems as if they'll never stop. I remain standing in the same spot; the deeply felt wolf song holds me in place. I can't hold back the tears now—the way the two wolves express their mourning is overwhelming.

Wolf howls can sound very different depending on the situation. Through the pitch, volume, and rhythm of their voices, the pack can communicate happiness, excitement, confusion, insecurity, fear, or other emotions. The animals can voice completely different melodies in different circumstances.

Nevertheless, Flocke and Nanuk cannot grasp the finality of death. After weeks, and at every opportunity, they watch the approach of the red car that took Chinook away, as if they still hope that it will bring their companion back. They don't let themselves be diverted by food or affection. Similar behavior toward a dead pack member can be observed among a wild wolf pack. When a female wolf starves from malnourish-

ment in the winter, the rest of her pack returns to her for many days and tries to get her to stand up by prodding her with their noses. Solid connections form in a wolf pack; the death of a companion brings inevitable emotions and many changes in the complicated pack structure.

◼ A New Equality: Protection and Respect

In the past, people always tried to deny that animals had feelings comparable to human emotions. The Christian thinker Thomas Aquinas (1225–1274) denied that either animals or women had souls. And a couple of hundred years later, the philosopher and Jesuit student René Descartes (1596–1650) called animals mere chattel and classified them as soulless machines devoid of reason. They were denied every right, and humans were allowed to inflict suffering, pain, and worse upon them at any time.

People and animals live in a paradoxical relationship. Animals are treated as creatures similar to us, carriers of culture, and household members with their own rights; but they are also used as objects for breeding, experimentation, and food.

In recent decades society has changed its thinking. The protection of animals has been incorporated into law. It has been unequivocally declared that all animals are our fellow creatures whose lives and well-being must be protected. Humans are still allowed to use animals for their needs, but only in responsible ways in accordance with the valid legal requirements of animal protection. No one may hurt an animal or inflict suffering or damage without justification; animals must be fed appropriately for their species, cared for reasonably, and housed humanely.

Admittedly, animals don't have a legal position of their own comparable to humans, but modern laws offer them—in theory at least—a certain protection.

Animal Friendships and Birds Associated with Wolves

In our game park there are two different wolf subspecies: the white tundra wolves who live in the Arctic and the far north of Canada, and the black timber wolves from the forests of North America. We are still missing the European gray wolf. After careful consideration, we've decided to provide a home for this species in our park as well.

Since gray wolves are by nature extremely wary of people, we decide to get week-old pups and rear them ourselves. Hand-reared wolves quickly get used to a new enclosure and people passing by. When they flee, they don't go far, so visitors can watch and photograph these animals without disturbing them.

■ Two Wolf Pups and a Fawn

We order two pups from a Bavarian animal park. We know that they're due to be born around mid-May, and everything necessary for rearing them is ready at our home weeks ahead of time: special milk, little bottles with different nipples, a scale for regular monitoring of weight, blankets, and a plastic container with somewhat high sides to hold them their first days, as well as a pile of paper towels for the essential belly massage. The mother wolf licks the bellies of her pups, thereby stimulating metabolism and digestion; since I would naturally like to spare myself this experience, I prefer to use paper towels. I can hardly wait for the arrival of my new charges.

On a Friday evening, I get a phone call from a woman in the neighboring village: "Ms. Askani, my children found a fawn in the woods this afternoon, petted her, and eventually brought her home with them. They thought her mother had abandoned her. Now the little one is lying here and I don't know what to do with her!" I often get phone calls like this in the springtime. During the day, the cute little hares, squirrels, martens, or foxes are usually gathered up out of ignorance, and in the evening people ask themselves the question, "What do I do with it?" Since the little wolves are to come soon and will need me around the clock for the

Tanja's mixed "nursery."

first weeks, leaving me almost no time for anything else, I've planned to take in no other bottle babies this year. But the woman tells me that the little foundling has not yet had anything to eat or drink, and it becomes clear to me that she needs help fast. Tomorrow could be too late. Since I have all the necessities ready in my house, I decide to take care of the little one and pass her on to an animal keeper the following day.

Less than half an hour later, I have the tiny fawn in a big cardboard box in the house. She must be only a few hours old. Her umbilical cord is not even dry; it still feels like flesh. Late into the night, I try repeatedly to give her a bottle, but it doesn't work. She resists and spits the nipple out over and over. I give her a little time to calm down and then try again. Usually, young animals need two to three days to get used to the plastic nipple and learn the right sucking technique. With my every attempt to feed her, the fawn swallows a few drops of milk, more by mistake than anything, so that in the end, about half of the lifesaving liquid lands in her stomach. For today, we've done it. I don't sense that at the very same time on the same night, far away in a deep, freshly dug den, four newborn wolf pups are trying to reach their mother's milk for the first time.

I name the little fawn Linda. Within two days, she is quite at home

Only when they feel safe do the fawn and her wolf brothers step out of the protection of the spruce trees.

Opposite: Linda asserts herself best when eating.

with us. When she's hungry, she makes a high squealing sound until I appear with the bottle. After the feeding, she follows me throughout the house and assists me with my housework. When I need to leave, she stays motionless in her cardboard box and waits there until I come back. This behavior is innate for young deer. They do the same in the wild when separated from their mothers. The mother comes back only a couple of times a day to let the young one drink and then disappears again to avoid making predators aware of her offspring. Fawns have almost no scent of their own during their first weeks and are best protected from predators when they remain still in their hiding place.

Linda proves herself to be a problem-free bottle child, and so the time comes to give her to the animal caretaker in the park. But one problem remains: she will only nurse the bottle with me. She refuses the food from anyone else, even my husband. She won't let anyone but me get close to her.

When we can finally pick up our wolf pups, I have no choice but to put Linda and her cardboard box in the back seat of the car and take her with us on the nearly nine-hundred-mile-long trip. Along the way, I occasionally stop at a gas station to fill up and take care of Linda. She takes it easy, drinking her milk ration and disappearing again into the box. Presum-

ably, she's the only fawn from Lower Saxony who has ever traveled by car to Bavaria.

Shortly after midnight, we reach our destination. As arranged, we ring the bell to get the custodian of the animal park out of bed. He soon appears with an animal transport cage in which two pups the size of guinea pigs whimper. They're about ten days old. We name them Daylight and Shadow.

Not half an hour later, we're back on the road heading home with all three young animals. I start thinking: how will it go with the fawn and the wolves? In no more than three weeks, the pups will begin exploring their surroundings and start romping around and fighting. Play has an important function for all young animals. They use it to prepare themselves for the life ahead of them; play fosters skills and stamina and establishes boundaries. Linda demonstrates this principle mostly late in the afternoon when she does her rounds in the yard so intensively that she can hardly catch her breath. In this way, she prepares her muscles, lungs, and circulation for the future necessity of fleeing for her life. Day by day, she gets faster and more skilled, and her stamina grows visibly. She has long since left her cardboard box and moves freely through the house and yard. She follows me all day long, so I cannot prevent her from repeatedly encountering the wolf pups. But when I drive to work, she immediately hides herself in the reeds at the edge of the pond, lying there quietly until I appear again at home. At night she comes into the house and shares the dog basket on the floor of the bedroom with our dachshund Drossel.

Soon the wolf pups are four weeks old. I have long since swapped the plastic box where they spent their first days for a bigger cardboard box. The latter would only fit through the door folded up and now almost fills the living room. Only in this way do I have the pups somewhat under control when I am out of the house, and they have enough space to romp

around. They get more and more mobile, and I take them into the yard as often as possible so they can fulfill their desire to play.

Before now, I've only reared one pup at a time. This is the first time I have a "twin pack" of them at home, and I'm certainly worried about how our property will look when two rascals unleash their destructive energies. Flocke and Nanuk have made me somewhat accustomed to their notion of "yard work." To my surprise, though, this time everything is very different. The pups are so busy with each other that it hardly occurs to them to commit other kinds of foolishness. We don't have to put up electric wires on the windows or a board on the door to protect our house. And the yard is barely damaged; the pups are satisfied with digging a couple of holes. Even so, to be on the safe side, we protect a couple of corners that are important to us, such as our pond and flowerbed, with a wire fence.

Now the pups are almost six weeks old, and their games are getting rougher and rougher. They fight and shake each other by the nape of the neck and roll around on the ground. Their thinly furred bellies are scarred from wounds they give each other with their sharp milk teeth. I also find two little wounds on Linda's neck. She doesn't find it the least bit fun when a pup hangs onto her leg or neck; she can't understand such games at all. She is faster than they are, however, and when they get to be too much for her, she rescues herself from their high spirits with a couple of leaps. Our yard is big enough that she can get out of their way. But instead of avoiding them, Linda seeks out contact with the clumsy pups again and

Above: Between playtimes, the little ones sleep. For pups, bodily contact is very important.

Opposite: At six weeks old, the little ones' games get rougher and rougher.

again. Daily, I watch all three of the little ones sniff each other and lick each other's snouts. When they get scared, they flee together and look for protection in the thick spruces at the edge of the yard. When the supposed danger is over, they slowly come out together and look cautiously in all directions. Nevertheless, I doubt that this friendship can last much longer. The pups develop incredibly fast; day by day they become faster, more skilled, and more resourceful. Besides that, they eat a huge amount of meat every day, and right now deer meat is at the top of their menu. When I watch how they greedily attack the chunks of meat, I fear that they will soon greet me at the gate without Linda, but with round bellies.

For this reason, we split the yard in half with a fence. One side is intended for the wolves, and the wolf-free zone belongs to Linda. They are to stay separated, at least during times when no one is home. Before I drive to work the next day, I sort the young animals: the meat-eating pups in the left half and the plant-eating fawn in the right half of the yard. To my surprise, when I come home two hours later, I find all of them peacefully together again. Linda has joined the two little wolves, and a big bunch of hair on her neck has been scratched away. Was it the wolves? I look at the fence for weak spots. Where could she jump over it? Quickly, I find something; her hair clings to the top part of the fence.

Cuddling can quickly become serious. The young wolves learn to measure the power of their bites through pain.

She probably tried to get out of her "safe zone" several times, losing the hair on the wire in the process. In a compromise, I lower one part of the fence somewhat in the hope that if Linda needs to she can rescue herself from her siblings with a leap into her safe zone. The coming days show that she actually makes use of both halves of the yard. But not to protect herself from wolf attacks. Instead, she uses her side of the yard over and over again to reach the juicy bamboo shoots at the back along the pond.

It is the end of July, a hot summer. The temperature climbs to 104 degrees during the day. In this heat, our yard seems empty and abandoned. No animal chooses to lie in the blazing sun the way people do. The three-month-old pups spend most of their daylight hours panting in the shade. They postpone all of their activities until late afternoon and night. In the early morning hours and at twilight, when it gets cooler, Linda comes out to graze as well.

Around nine o'clock in the evening, when the sun is very low, the pups' hours of play usually start. It gets unbelievably intense. It almost appears as if the pups have to make up for the enforced quiet of many hours. They fight unrestrainedly, shake each other, and run away again until one of them falls or brings the other one down, without regard for injuries. During this time, Linda is like a forest ghost. She is neither seen nor heard; I can only guess that she is hiding somewhere, watching the wolf games. She has learned that this is more prudent than taking part in these wild evening romps. She notices right away, though, when it gets quieter. Then she suddenly appears and begins her own game: she runs around the yard repeatedly and at great speed. The pups immediately stop fighting, and, taken aback, sit down to watch her. They look left, right, left, right, as though watching a tennis match. As Linda runs past them the fifth time, they jump up and try to hunt her down. But by the time they run after her for a couple of yards, she overtakes them from behind. They are totally confused, sit down side by side again and look right and left, as if they think there are at least five other Lindas jumping around in the yard.

After the three young animals have gotten the roughhousing out of their systems, it gets downright loving. Long-legged Linda bends over

There are animal friendships that transcend species boundaries.

the pups and sniffs them from their noses to the tips of their tails. The pups then roll on their backs and reach for her very tenderly with their front paws. Eventually, Linda takes two steps to the side and starts grazing. The young wolves watch her intently. Her preference for greens appears to make them somewhat suspicious. After a while they get up and creep up on her with their noses in the air and ears raised. They snap at the half-chewed blades of grass with their front teeth and try to pull them out of Linda's mouth. When they are successful, they chew on the grass a little themselves but then spit everything out, quite disappointed. They watch the strange eating habits of their "little sister" with tilted heads. If they have a bone or piece of meat themselves, they growl at Linda as soon as she comes too close to them. They don't want to share their meal with anyone.

But Linda is first to get to the bottle. She has an amazing ability to assert herself against the young wolves and employs every possible trick to get them away from it. To give the wolves any milk at all, I have to make sure Linda is full first.

◼ Wolves and a Falcon

There is an area in our yard where the grass is somewhat higher. We occasionally keep a few raptors there. Usually, we have first trained these birds with falconry. They then require more intensive training until they can take part in flight presentations. Here, they grow accustomed to people, dogs, and passing cars, an important prerequisite for their future work in front of the public. Right now, a saker falcon named Luna is staying here. Daylight and Shadow, now six weeks old, have discovered for themselves the place originally intended for the raptors. From its rise, they have a good overview of the property. At first, Luna was not enthusiastic about their presence, however, and reacted somewhat nervously. But after a couple of days, she simply ignores the two of them. The pups have paid almost no attention to her beyond a brief and cautious sniff at first.

From the beginning of their fourth week, the pups receive a bowl of finely chopped meat in addition to their usual meal of milk. They greedily devour the meat on the porch. Three weeks later, I offer each of them a larger piece of meat so they can train their chewing muscles. The pups snap up a morsel, but instead of eating it on the porch as usual, they carry it up to the rise, their favorite place. The falcon notices this immediately, of course, pounces on the first arriving pup and rips his food out of his mouth. The pup is uninjured, but the flapping falcon has put a powerful scare into him. Within a few minutes, though, the pup ventures out of his hiding place and tries to take back his piece of meat. He creeps up on the falcon, who has already begun to eat. As the falcon discovers the pup crawling toward her, she cackles threateningly and immediately covers the stolen meat with her wings. After a while, the pup gives up and watches the falcon devour her meal from a safe distance.

This experience does not prevent both pups from carrying their pieces of meat up to their favorite spot next to the falcon to eat it there. So in the following days, one or two hunks of meat change ownership again and again. The falcon maintains the upper hand but only for a short time. Just a week after the first theft, I can see both young wolves carefully watching the bird until they get an opportunity to take back the piece of meat. This often happens with teamwork: one of the pups distracts the falcon from the side and the other rips the meat out of the surprised bird's talons. Day by day, the young wolves get more self-assured and skilled. Soon they no longer need to defend their own meat; on the contrary, they miss no chance to steal the bird's food. Their jealousy over

Shadow and Daylight try to take food from the saker falcon, Luna.

food is so great that they even steal it when they're not hungry at all, carrying the stolen meat away only to let it lie. Ultimately, I have to guard the falcon at feeding time so that she gets enough to eat.

A digesting falcon emits certain sounds. It's amazing how fast the pups understand the connection between these sounds and eating. Even the quietest falcon sound pulls them right out of a deep sleep. They jump up wide awake and run directly to the bird to take her ration away. It isn't hunger that drives them both; it's more an endless desire to play. In the wild, this ability to understand and correctly identify various sounds and events comes in handy for wolves.

■ Wolves and Ravens

Cooperation in finding food can be very helpful, especially in winter, when many animals suffer from hunger and struggle to survive.

Observations indicate that wolves have a very special relationship with ravens. The two species form an expedient community; where there are wolves, ravens are not far away. These highly intelligent birds, also often called "wolf birds," specialize in finding carrion. They are the first to discover an animal's carcass, often only a few hours after it has died. They are not equipped to penetrate the thick skin of large mammals to get to the meat, but their excited calls attract wolves, who will open the body with their powerful fangs and eat until satisfied. Afterward, enough meat remains for the ravens, so both species profit from the find. Ravens also watch for suitable prey and reveal the location of injured or sick animals. They sometimes even attack the prey to make the hunt easier for the wolves.

Ravens often build their nests near a wolf den. The development of both animals is very compatible. Right after leaving the den for the first time, wolf pups hear the loud caws of the young ravens begging for food. In the fall, the wolf pups move into their territory with their parents, and the young ravens become self-sufficient, too. So even in the period of their development, the two kinds of animals truly make an impression on each other.

Ravens share the same fate as the wolves. They have long been persecuted by people as competitors for prey and were nearly exterminated since the invention of firearms. Today in the European Union, they are specially protected and hunting them is not allowed.

To the Native Americans, ravens and wolves are animals of wisdom. In Native American legends, Raven created the sun, moon, stars, and finally humans. In Germanic sagas, wolves and ravens often appear together. The highest god Odin is accompanied by two ravens and two wolves. Every morning, he sends out his two ravens Hugin (thought) and

Wolves can interpret the excited calls of the raven very precisely.

Munin (memory) to survey the world. Upon their return, they report to him what they have seen on their flights. For this reason, Odin is also called the "raven god." He views the entire world from his throne and at his feet the wolves Freki (greed) and Geri (gluttony) stand guard. The Odin saga preserves the primeval wisdom of our past and speaks of the connection between the hunter, the wolf, and the raven.

Wolves and ravens are not only found together in the wild and in old traditions. In the winter months, the enclosures of zoos and game parks are often besieged by wild ravens. Our game park is no exception; they are magically attracted to our wolf pack. Nevertheless, our wolves don't think much of them. When swarms of ravens land in the wolf enclosure in the evenings to grab leftover food, they don't enjoy the same freedom to do as they please that they would in the wild. For the wolves, these visitors' presence is a welcome opportunity to test their own skill, speed, and cunning at hunting birds. The wolves are repeatedly successful at catching and killing inexperienced ravens, though they don't eat them afterward. A dead raven is not seen as food but as a "toy." Wolves born and kept in captivity have never experienced extreme hunger or what the hunt for survival means. Nor can they discover the advantages of forming a hunting community with ravens.

The wolf pups Daylight and Shadow are three months old and big enough to finally leave our yard and move into the park. They have already accompanied me there on occasion for a few hours to get accustomed to their new surroundings. Today, I come home without the

Wild wolves and ravens form a hunting community.

wolves for the first time. It is an odd feeling, even when I know that they're doing well in the game park. I clean up the yard, collect the remaining bones and toys from the grass, take down the temporary protective fence, and fill in the holes dug by the pups. Linda is right on my heels during all of this work.

Gradually it gets dark. I sit with my husband on the porch; it's strangely quiet. For the first time in quite a while, we don't have to keep the porch door closed to eat our supper without a wolf showing up at the table. Linda behaves differently today. Though she has already had her evening bottle, she appears unsettled. She jumps back and forth in the yard, then takes advantage of the open doors and runs squealing past us into the house. But she doesn't calm down there, either. She systematically examines each room. She leaps through the kitchen, through my workroom, and lands in the bathtub. It takes nearly three days for Linda to give up her search.

I have to admit that I underestimated the animal friendship that developed between the young wolves and the fawn. I thought that when the pups had disappeared from our yard, Linda would finally have enough space for herself. I never would have thought that she would miss the "wild bunch" so much.

■ Animal Friendships That Transcend Species Boundaries

There are, in fact, friendships among animals that transcend species boundaries. An extreme example of such a bond between two completely different species occurred with a wild lioness from Samburu National Park in Kenya. She adopted a young oryx antelope and even allowed its biological mother to visit it regularly and feed it. Amazing films were made of this odd relationship. After some time, unfortunately, the little antelope was killed by a young male lion. But the lioness didn't give up and found herself a new antelope fawn.

In a zoo in Thailand's Chonburi Province, the female tiger Sai Mai also has downright curious friends. She plays with piglets in her enclosure. In the first four months of her life, the now-adult tiger was nursed and reared by a domestic pig. Consequently, she regards the grunting fellow occupants of her enclosure not as tasty prey, but as her own siblings.

Another unusual animal friendship became well known in German-speaking countries. One day a stray black cat appeared in the Asiatic black bear's enclosure at the Berlin Zoo. No one knew where she had come from and no one believed that she would survive there for long. But the little house tiger and the old she-bear hit it off right away. From the first day, the two were inseparable. Now they share food and a sleeping spot; they cuddle and sunbathe together. This harmonious living situation has lasted a number of years.

Numerous polar bears roam near the city of Churchill on Hudson Bay in Canada every fall, waiting for the bay to freeze so they can wander farther north. These largest land predators hunt everything that they can get their paws on. The Eskimos' tied-down sled dogs often count as polar bears' favorite prey—but not always in Churchill. There, a bear has been coming right into the city for years to romp around with a dog. And there are four more bears who regularly visit the sled dogs. Even polar bear experts can't find an explanation for this phenomenon. Things often happen in nature that we do not understand.

Dogs with Wolf Blood

One February evening I get a phone call from a stranger. "Excuse me for bothering you so late," he says, "but I've heard that you know wolves well. I have a question for you, and maybe you can help me. I was in the United States on business last month. I bought a wolf pup there and brought it home with me. Is it possible to somehow determine if it is actually a purebred wolf?"

A wolf pup at this time of year? I get somewhat suspicious and ask, "How old is the little one?" "Three months," answers the man, and he describes what the pup looks like, how it is developing, and how it behaves. We have a long conversation, and almost everything points to this being no ordinary dog pup, but a young wolf. But the fact remains that in February there are no wolf pups; that's when the breeding season begins.

The wild relatives of dogs only bear young once a year. South of the forty-fifth parallel, wolf pups come into the world between the middle of March and April. North of there, they are born between April and the end of May. Therefore, I arrive at the conclusion that this man's pup is most likely a hybrid wolf. Since even pups from the same litter can look very different, it is only possible to prove whether it is a mixed-blood or purebred wolf with a DNA test. I am aware that buying a wolf or hybrid wolf in the United States is no problem, though laws against keeping and breeding these animals have been passed in many states after several difficult incidents involving children.

■ Random Crosses and Breeding Trials

Half-breed wolves—crosses between a dog and a wolf—have always been around, wanted or unwanted, especially in regions where dogs and wolves can encounter each other unsupervised, such as in Alaska with sled dogs. There, in exceptional cases, but repeatedly and without human intervention, wolves mate with dogs. Generally, these cases involve a passing female wolf and a male dog.

In Germany's Muskauer Heath, there was an uproar in 2003 when it

Although the Czechoslovakian wolfhound (left) is part wolf, the difference between it and a wolf (right) is clearly visible, especially in the teeth.

was determined that the four offspring of a wild wolf showed great similarities to a dog. Since these hybrid offspring can mate with wolves, the genetic purity of the small wolf population in Germany could become seriously endangered. For this reason, two of the pups were captured and kept in an enclosure. But the other two disappeared without a trace.

Various breeding experiments are conducted intentionally in the naïve belief that a "super dog" can be bred from a wolf and a dog. For these purposes, half-breed wolves are differentiated from hybrid wolves. A half-breed wolf is a first-generation cross between a purebred wolf and a domestic dog. A hybrid wolf is the second (or even further removed) generation resulting from a cross between two wolf hybrids or a wolf hybrid and a domestic dog.

Experience with dogs is not sufficient for handling such animals. The possibly fatal combination of the wild and domestic causes half-breeds to be much more unpredictable and aggressive than purebred wolves. An animal with the predatory instincts of the wolf may result, but without the wolf's sensitivity, reluctance to bite, or fear and respect for people. The first serious problems usually appear when the animal is sexually mature. The wild inheritance of hybrids suddenly breaks through in the second or third year of life, at the latest. They attempt to gain the highest position in their human pack, and primitive inborn behaviors are called forth much faster and executed with more consequence than among dogs. Their attachment to the people they grew up with and their shyness toward strangers make it impossible to pass them on to a new,

113

more suitable owner. Unfortunately, killing the animal is often the only responsible way out.

Nevertheless, some people regard wolves, half-breed wolves, or hybrid wolves as a status symbol or as a tangible symbol of wildness. Even the old Iranian book *Avesta*, which tells of the creation of the world, warns against crosses between dogs and wolves and calls them "a sin committed against the dog." It must be added: not only against the dog but also against the wolf.

Opposite: Calmness and aggressiveness. Wolves possess a wide range of emotions that are undesirable and inappropriate for a dog.

The first serious breeding experiments took place about thirty years ago in the United States and Canada. A wolf was crossed with a sled dog to obtain dogs with greater stamina and power, and higher resistance to disease. Without the expected outcome, though. At first, mostly the northern breeds such as the Siberian husky, malamute, and Samoyed were mated with wolves. Later, dozens of other breeds were tried. The German shepherd was not spared such experiments, either. It was intentionally crossed with the wolf many times at the beginning of the twentieth century, mainly to improve its appearance. People hoped that the German shepherd would retain certain anatomical characteristics of wolves, such as small, erect ears and a heavily furred, hanging tail. Other goals were improved agility and greater stamina. But this attempt failed as well. The animals were extremely shy of people, easily scared, mistrusting, and eager to bite as soon as they felt cornered.

Despite these failures, dog breeders were repeatedly fascinated by the beauty, strength, grace, intelligence, and character of wolves. They tried, with the help of wolves, to breed a "better" dog, and ultimately two new dog breeds arose, the Czechoslovakian wolfhound and the Saarloos wolfhound.

In 1933 Karel Hartel laid the foundation for the creation of the Czechoslovakian wolfhound. In the name of science, he mated the Carpathian wolf Britta with the German shepherd Cesar z Brisoveho Haje. The objective was to gain knowledge about the heredity of certain maternal characteristics in offspring. In 1958, a young wolfhound (an ancestor in the direct line of the wolf Britta and the shepherd Cesar) was made a guard dog with the Czech border patrol. Through this event came the

idea to establish a new breed of dog. In 1966, the breeders applied for entry in the breed book of the Fédération Cynologique Internationale (FCI). The application was rejected, however, and interest in the breed sank. Only in 1982 was the Czechoslovakian wolfhound finally recognized as the new national dog breed. Thereafter, sixty-six dogs were registered in the FCI breed book. All purebred dogs must complete a performance exam during which adult animals run thirty miles and young dogs run fifteen miles.

The outer resemblance of the Czechoslovakian wolfhound to the wolf is unmistakable: the elastic gait; the silver-gray coat; small, erect, triangular ears; the relatively narrow, yellow eyes; and canine teeth that are very large for a dog. It barks much less than other dogs; instead it typically howls. It's distant toward strangers, but not hostile. By no means is it a dog for the city.

The second dog breed with wolf blood is easily confused with a wolf and is even sometimes difficult for experts to distinguish: the Dutch Saarloos wolfhound. This breed is named for its breeder, the Dutchman Leendert Saarloos. He was convinced that the dog had lost too much of its natural behavior; it was too domesticated for him, and in his eyes, had degenerated too much. In the 1920s, to breed his "ideal dog," he crossed the female wolf Fleur with the German shepherd Gerard van de Fransenum. He repeated this combination numerous times with the hope of

Above left: Two Czechoslovakian wolfhounds.

Above right: A wolf-German shepherd cross.

Opposite: Like wolves, Czechoslovakian wolfhounds also feel most at home in a pack.

creating his "natural dog" through strict selection. Many of the pups died of distemper since Saarlos wanted to breed "naturally healthy" dogs and therefore rejected immunizations. His assumption that his wolf-hounds would become resistant to infectious diseases was not confirmed. His breeder wolf Fleur starved due to a viral illness. Afterward, a zoo gave him a second female wolf, Fleur II, whom Saarlos also used for his breeding experiments.

He was not satisfied with his results. The newly bred dogs were shy and unreliable in their relations with people. The attempt to train them as police dogs failed. Training them as rescue dogs was just as unsuccessful. Nor were they useful as watchdogs, since they seldom barked. But through an accident in his family, Saarloos believed that he had discovered a possible use for his dogs. As his wife, who had sup-ported his work, went blind, he attempted to train his dogs as Seeing Eye dogs. When one example of the new breed succeeded with this test, Saarlos believed that he had been proven correct and opened a school for Seeing Eye dogs. It soon became clear, however, that the new breed of dog was fundamentally unsuited for this training. Its shy and cautious behavior made dependable service on heavily traveled streets nearly impossible.

Leendert Saarloos died in 1969 without having found his "dream dog." The Saarloos-wolfhound was officially recognized in the Nether-lands six years later.

Less well-known than the two recognized wolfhound breeds is the Italian wolfhound, Lupo Italiano. It is extremely active and therefore

especially well suited for use as a rescue dog during natural catastrophes. The first breeding experiments occurred in 1966.

Wolfhounds are not dogs for beginners. Anyone wishing to have such a dog should first become well-informed about their nature and needs, and only get pups from experienced breeders.

■ The Superior Strength of Instincts

Today, it is questionable whether there are still defensible reasons to cross a dog with a wolf. What do you hope for from an animal that is neither dog nor wolf?

According to the newest genetic findings, it required at least fifty thousand years of development to produce today's dog: eager, willing, able to subordinate itself, and easily trainable. For a hybrid wolf to behave like a dog, most of its wolf characteristics must be removed through complex breeding measures.

Since the domestic dog is fully integrated into human society, its capabilities can be utilized in many areas. Even a tame wolf, on the other hand, is difficult to influence and follows its natural instincts. Of course, wolves are very intelligent, and it's relatively easy to teach them little tricks. They quickly grasp that they can secure a reward by following a command. Nevertheless, they ultimately decide whether to follow a command or not, according to their instinct. The ability to decide quickly and without a mistake is crucial for their survival in the wild. So it's hardly possible to expect a "trained" wolf to guard a flock of sheep or, like a watchdog, attack only upon command.

A wolf seldom barks. A short "wuff" is sufficient to warn pups about danger, for example. A dog, in contrast, makes itself noticeable by barking in situations when a wolf never would. Every dog owner can recognize the reason for a bark. A dog barks happily over the arrival of a familiar person, and differently when a stranger appears. With a hunting dog, you can recognize whether it has treed a cat or a squirrel by the rhythm, length, volume, and pitch of its barking.

For a dog to work dependably with a person, it must be free of fear and the tendency to flee, which could never be expected of a wolf. For wolves, fleeing from danger is a necessity. Also, wolves and hybrid wolves can't be house-trained since they want to mark their territory. And their unstoppable curiosity can quickly become a disaster for their owner. Everything is examined with teeth; as a rule, both yard and household will be demolished beyond recognition in a very short time. In addition, wolves are true escape artists. To keep such an animal, you need extra-high fences and a grate sunk into the ground. Their inborn instinct to hunt, which even in hunting dogs has been greatly reduced through breeding, can become a serious danger to house pets. Even children can unleash hunting behavior relatively easily.

There are roughly four hundred registered dog breeds and an astronomically high number of mixed breeds. Anyone who isn't able to find a suitable dog for themselves among these should preferably bypass owning a dog altogether.

My telephone conversation with the new owner of the "wolf pup" is long, and I grow genuinely curious. The man promises to visit me in the coming days with his charge. I inform him that such animals are subject to the Washington Convention on International Trade in Endangered Species of Wild Flora and Fauna, and that an official license and so-called certificate of origin are required to possess them. I probably make him feel uncertain, and despite our arranged meeting I wait in vain for him and his "young wolf."

With his impressive teeth, Nanuk could crush Tanja's face. That he only pinches lightly is a special sign of wolf tenderness.

Wolf and Human

Homo sapiens, the "human" species, belongs to the hominid family together with the anthropoid apes. Nevertheless, the lifestyles of human and wolf are much more similar than the lifestyles of humans and apes.

The oldest known human remains, found in 3.5-million-year-old deposits in East Africa, show that Homo sapiens developed from earlier human species. It is well-known that humans and chimpanzees are genetically very similar. Even though there are millions of differences in the structure of their molecules, their inherited substance is 98.7 percent similar. Despite this genetic closeness, the paths of the two species diverge over the course of evolution. As a result of their further development, humans become a "predatory ape." As hunters, they depend on a bigger territory than their plant-eating ape relatives. They leave the forest walking upright, their social structure changes, and they develop into group hunters with a fixed hierarchy and complex communication structure.

Their well-planned and -organized hunting methods enable them, alone among primates, to kill prey much larger than themselves.

A plant eater must take in a relatively large amount of food to satisfy its energy needs. To absorb the nutrients, the plant food must be well chewed and chopped up. So a plant eater spends much of its time daily grazing, eating, and chewing. A meat eater, on the other hand, can absorb high-value food in concentrated form relatively quickly and so can use the rest of its time for resting, wandering, and nurturing social contacts.

Dominant wolves demonstrate their position with body posture and a raised tail.

■ Early Domestication

It has long been assumed that the wolf was domesticated by humans about fourteen thousand years ago. There are different theories about how this happened. One of these supposes that humans reared a wolf pup and thereby made it imprint on them.

Recently, an experiment in California with dog paw prints found in a cave in Chauvet, France, determined that they are at least 25,000 years old. These paw prints are clearly different from a wolf's, which proves that dogs and wolves developed genetic differences much earlier than has previously been assumed. A genotype analysis led by Swedish and American evolutionary biologists concludes that the domestication of the wolf must have happened between 135,000 and 60,000 years ago.

The first early humans migrated from Africa, their land of origin, to Asia only ninety thousand years ago. This means that wolf domestication could have begun before the beginning of this migration. It involved not only the simple taming of the wild animal, but also a whole series of complex biological and behavioral changes. According to DNA analysis, wolves and early humans lived together for more than five thousand generations before the emergence of so-called civilized societies and cultures.

■ Wolf Pack and Family Unit

The lifestyle of ancient primitive cultures strongly resembles that of a wolf pack. Both live in small family groups containing multiple generations, with a fixed hierarchal structure and precise distribution of labor according to gender. To enable group living, humans, like wolves, pos-

sess well-developed social behavior and form strong relationships with the other members of the family unit or pack, respectively. Their great intelligence, ability to learn, instinctive sensitivity, and consistent loyalty play important roles in this social cohesion. Wolves and humans stand together as meat eaters at the top of the food chain; they possess the same territories and hunt the same prey animals. The primates that are genetically related to humans, however, remain with the other plant eaters a step below them.

It is very likely that wolves were not nearly as shy in earlier times as we know them to be today. A meeting of human and wolf then, or possible cooperation during the hunt, could have been much less complicated than we think of it today. Over time, animals acquire anxiety, fear, and shyness when relating to people. Practicing generations of senseless persecution, humans exterminate all creatures not cautious enough to get out of their way in time. Only the shyest of them avoid this fate and can survive, reproduce, and pass these characteristics on to their offspring. The shy European fox and its close relative, the tundra fox, are often mentioned as examples of this. But in the unutilized, uninhabited areas where the tundra fox lives, it could not be so intensively hunted and persecuted as the red fox native to our region, and so the tundra fox is naturally more trusting than our fox. For the same reason, large differences in behavior can be detected among European and Arctic wolves despite their close kinship.

Everyone knows from experience how much a house pet can influence a person's behavior. Regardless of whether it's an old lady's budgie or a little girl's rabbit, every animal influences our lives, our daily routine, and our habits. Animals adapt to human needs and vice versa. And how was it back then, when the paths of wolves and early humans crossed in the wilderness and they first had contact with each other? Certainly, our ancestors' constant contact with primitive dogs strongly affected the further development of both and led, through a long process of mutual influence and interaction, to the evolution of humans and dogs. The connection between the two species gained increasing meaning and consistency, and as a result a kind of symbiosis new in evolutionary history arose.

▇ Similarities between Wolves and Humans

Evolution marched steadily forward and humans distanced themselves more and more from animal behaviors, instead categorizing themselves as unique and enlightened. Their lives became increasingly dominated by requirements, rules, laws, and regulations. All human behaviors now deemed typical originated through a long learning process. Despite this, primitive survival instincts from hunting and gathering times still exist, however well hidden.

Today, numerous similarities between humans and wolves can still be found through close observation. For example, wolves display very similar expressive behavior. With their body language and facial expressions, which can change according to the situation, both species can send clear and easily comprehensible signals. A submissive posture, such as a lowered head and evasive look, has an aggression-inhibiting effect on an attacker under normal conditions. A military officer's showy epaulettes and gold braids have the same meaning as the dignified, raised tail of the alpha wolf. We line our national borders with boundary markers and our own property with a fence. A wolf does the same but simply uses a different method; it marks its territory with urine and excrement. The borders are strictly

guarded; when an uninvited guest enters a marked area, humans and wolves react equally aggressively.

Countless other similarities can be found.

Whether in the workplace or in school, bullying is a recurring issue these days. Social hierarchy, as seen in a wolf pack, is behind this.

Issues surrounding offspring also show parallels; as with wolves, children have a special status in human families. Grandparents, aunts, and other relatives are charmed by the little ones, care for them, and offer well-meaning advice about rearing. Whether human or wolf, the reaction is the same. When a small child starts to cry, relatives turn worriedly toward him or her to see if they can help.

During mating season, wolves don't lose sight of each other for a second—not unlike people in this phase—playing and dancing with each other and putting their front paws on each other's shoulders and touching noses. Tender mouth contact and intensive touching are exchanged ceaselessly. The beloved partner is jealously guarded; every competitor who nears is mercilessly driven away.

Despite advanced civility, our "wolflike" hunting instinct has not yet totally vanished either. The all-too-comfortably obtained vacuum-packed "prey" from the supermarket cannot quell our desire to hunt, so we take up other fields of activity: stalking deer with a camera or finding fulfillment in sports or play. It is interesting, by the way, that almost all popular computer games deal with hunting, mastering dangers, and solving specialized problems. And not least, I can't help but think of a wolf pack when I observe people's behavior at a hotel breakfast buffet, at a cold buffet at a party, or during seasonal bargain hunting.

■ Wolf Behavior and Human Behavior

A businessman informs me of his wish to hold a leadership workshop for a large company in front of our wolf enclosure.

How can you communicate something useful to managers about leading a business on the basis of small examples from wolf family life? Despite my skepticism, I consent, and we arrange a time. The businessman appears with a colorful mixture of men and women of varying ages,

Opposite: Easily comprehensible signals are sent with body language and facial expressions.

and we go to the enclosure together. On the way, I talk about our wolves; the mood lightens and the first questions come.

When we arrive at the enclosure, I gather from the wolves' behavior that they don't understand why I remain outside, in contrast to my custom, and a certain restlessness is apparent in them. They run along the fence and attempt to come as close as possible to me despite the metal that separates us. This doesn't happen without growling and flashing of teeth, of course. Their behavior awakens the interest of the seminar participants and more and more questions arise: Who is the pack leader with the last word? How are tensions released? Is there bullying among wolves? How do they communicate with each other? I try to answer with short, concrete stories and incidents from the life of our pack, and together we find more and more parallels to human behavior.

Even the way the dominant pup Daylight and his little brother Shadow resolve their conflicts resembles two human siblings who fight over a toy during the day but fall asleep peacefully together at night. The play of the two gray wolves sometimes looks dangerous, but they go everywhere together and when resting, one seeks the presence of the other. This can be applied to teamwork in the workplace, where people can argue vehemently and then find a peaceful and productive way to cooperate.

When there is growing tension in the pack, every wolf seeks a "lightning rod," just as we humans do. This is usually an animal with a lower position who helps defuse conflicts in the pack before they grow into larger problems. A similar dynamic occurs in a family. Frustration brought home from work, which has built up over the course of a day, needs an outlet, and as a result, meaningless small things cause conflicts. The tension is defused and the world put back in order only when the context has been recognized and the problem talked about.

During the mating season, the situation in the enclosure also parallels the business environment when more than a pure working relationship develops between two colleagues. A sexual relationship between two coworkers doesn't necessarily contribute to a good atmosphere. The affected parties are usually more concerned with themselves than

Opposite: Shadow and Daylight go everywhere together.

with the execution of their work tasks. Personal emotions interfere with business decisions. In contrast to wolves, humans suffer from the great disadvantage that their readiness to mate is not limited to three weeks a year.

I don't expect these businesspeople to be wolf specialists. They're city dwellers, after all, who otherwise don't have anything to do with animals. Still, their completely false idea that a well-functioning wolf pack has a dominant, despotic, and aggressive lone ruler who secures himself the top spot with brutality and raw violence completely surprises me. Certainly, a well-functioning form of cooperative living isn't possible without a certain authority; nevertheless, every individual needs the freedom to develop. So during my remarks, I place special emphasis on the attentiveness and many tender gestures that wolves exchange daily, on their gentle and smart forms of problem solving, on their solid connections and peaceful family life. The less energy a team invests in power struggles and aggression and the more loyalty and cooperation are valued, the more effectively it can arrive at its desired goal. This simple principle can be applied to all groups in society.

In conclusion, we're amazed to find that despite the cold, drizzly weather the planned half-hour presentation has stretched to two hours. Whether the managers actually derive insight from this for their daily work is difficult for me to judge. But everyone participating certainly takes a piece of wolf home with them in their hearts.

Life in the Pack Goes On

Integration into the Pack

When it is time for Shadow and Daylight to move into the game park, the question arises as to whether they should get their own enclosure right away or, preferably, grow up with the tundra wolves. I decide on the second choice. Admittedly, this isn't without risk, but I hope that Nanuk and Flocke will accept the two pups and then the little ones can grow up in a pack under natural conditions. Later, when they're adults and the time comes when they would part from their pack in the wild, the two gray wolves will get their own enclosure.

The first attempts to join the two parties take place in a meadow outside the park. Flocke behaves beautifully. She immediately throws herself at the pups in a friendly manner, makes herself smaller, wags her tail, and sniffs and licks them. She takes her role as aunt so seriously that during their very first meeting she regurgitates digested meat for the pups, which Shadow and Daylight greedily eat right away. Nanuk, on the other hand, doesn't know what to do in this situation. The pups awaken his curiosity, but when they approach him, he growls at them. His aggressiveness toward the pups intensifies so much due to his uncertainty that I have to intervene to protect them. The situation doesn't get any better during further encounters. As the time for the little wolves' final move into the game park nears, we have to erect a fence within the enclosure to separate Nanuk from the rest of the pack. This way, he can make eye contact with Flocke and the pups, but he can't threaten them.

■ Need for Retreat and Protection

The first evening the two pups curiously examine the enclosure right away under Flocke's supervision; everything appears to be fine. Not until the next morning do I see how fearfully the little ones react when visitors approach. The more people walk past or stop and watch, the more the pups panic. With curled-up tails they jump back and forth, panting and looking for a hole in the fence so they can flee the enclosure. I try to calm them, but they're so agitated that they don't even react to my call. I have never observed such panic attacks with Flocke or Nanuk. This behavior

Opposite: Fights over prey or social hierarchy seldom result in serious injuries.

Overleaf: Pack members' howling in unison strengthens the family group.

proves that not even growing up in a "human pack" can completely eliminate the inborn caution and extreme shyness of the European wolf.

These undesirable characteristics continually make it difficult to achieve relaxed contact with people. It's impossible, for example, to habituate the gray wolves to the car, although I've been taking them to the park from the time they were small. The short car ride is a strain for them and makes them very scared. And it doesn't help even when a trusted person rides along to calm them. Over time, their fear becomes an unsolvable problem, and to spare them this stressful situation we must go to our destination on foot. But a car ride causes Flocke and Nanuk no difficulties.

In the late afternoon, as the stream of visitors to the wolf enclosure slowly decreases, Shadow and Daylight squeeze themselves into a corner, completely exhausted and scared. They follow the activities on the other side of the fence with their tongues hanging. In contrast, Flocke appears to be totally uninterested. She lies in her favorite spot in the middle of the enclosure and rests with her eyes half closed.

The next morning a surprise awaits me: When I arrive, I see only the two tundra wolves in the enclosure. After searching the entire area, I find the pups in a deep burrow that Flocke has dug for them overnight. As the little ones hear my calls, they quickly come out to greet me but disappear back inside the den whenever they hear an unfamiliar sound. This new option of retreat provides the pups with increasingly more security. More and more often they dare to leave the den and go farther and farther away from it until they are finally so far that they can ignore the activity outside the enclosure. The stable and quiet behavior of the tundra wolves also serves as an example for the pups; it helps them to overcome their fears.

■ Socialization in the Pack

Like people, wolves go through a socialization process. As they grow into the social hierarchy of the pack, they learn rules and come to recognize what their place is. To refine their inborn abilities, they learn from older or more skilled companions and try out important behaviors through play.

Opposite: Wolves learn in the pack by watching and imitating.

Above left: From the beginning, Flocke takes over the role of adoptive mother.

Above right: In contrast to Flocke, Nanuk is more reserved during the first meeting with the pups.

Opposite: Shadow instinctively averts aggressive behavior from Nanuk with active demonstrations of humility.

Although parental care is inborn, wolves must learn a lot in addition. They can gather experience by observing the rearing of pups in the pack and use this in their later lives with their own families. Nanuk grew up as an only child, and pups have never been born in his current pack. He never had the opportunity to get to know a family community, so he's very overwhelmed by the new situation. Every day, I let him out of his separate enclosure; under my supervision, he's allowed to play with the pups. His behavior improves visibly. Little by little, he discovers the father role for himself, and we can finally take down the fence. Now Shadow and Daylight have the possibility to naturally learn all the rules of social coexistence for themselves.

At first, Flocke and Nanuk tolerate the little gray ones' wild games with amazing patience. The pups tease them, jerk on their ears, bite their tails, nibble and tousle their coats. The bigger and older the pups get, the pushier and ruder they get. Flocke then usually seeks a safe refuge on the roof of the wooden hut. Nanuk, on the other hand, attempts to control the little ones by growling and baring his teeth. If these threatening gestures are not taken seriously, he bites them on the nose. This is an effective teaching method; he doesn't seek to injure the high-spirited pups, only discipline them. He can estimate the strength of his bite with

great precision. The little ones yowl loudly every time they are bitten, but more from fright than pain. The restored quiet that follows is nevertheless short-lived; soon the wild play picks up where it left off.

◼ Eating Habits

Watching the wolf family eat is no less interesting. The pups pounce greedily on the meat without letting themselves be daunted by the adults. Nanuk usually tries to make his position clear by flashing his teeth and fiercely growling, but the little ones don't let themselves be intimidated and steal his piece out from under his nose faster than he can see them.

Flocke, on the other hand, takes the biggest piece of meat to her place on the roof to eat it undisturbed.

Some people claim that wolves' regurgitation of food for pups isn't completely voluntary. First, they say, the pups' humble or submissive gestures, such as pushing their noses in the corner of an adult's mouth, stimulates the adult to regurgitate chopped and digested food.

Nevertheless, I observe again and again how Flocke goes to the pups after devouring her portion and regurgitates the meat before the little ones can even begin to beg. Sometimes she feeds the pups even when they are already so full that they let the regurgitated meal lie untouched. I still observe this considerate behavior of Flocke's in the first months of winter, when at seven months Shadow and Daylight are almost fully grown.

Communication between Wolves and People

■ Reaction to Being Called by Name

Books on wolves repeatedly assert that wolves don't respond when you call them by name. It's difficult for me to explain how this prejudice originated. On the one hand, the wolf is represented as a highly intelligent predator. On the other hand, it is denied the simple ability to react to being called. Every house pet, whether cat or parakeet, will answer to its name if it receives enough contact and care from a person. Why should it be different with a wolf?

Wolves raised alone, in particular, such as Flocke or later Nanuk and Chinook, can recognize their names easily and respond accordingly. Of course, wolves are not dogs, and the final decision about whether they follow a human call remains theirs alone.

Shadow and Daylight grew up as siblings; therefore when you call one of them by name, both come running up. Each wants to be the first one to approach me—there could well be something edible as a reward. People would have the same problem with dog pups reared together; they also need a certain amount of time to find out which name belongs

Sometimes wolves need to cool off, too. The author goes for a swim with Nanuk.

to them. Shadow and Daylight mastered this ability at six months old.

In the spring, just after I had picked up the pups, a television team got in touch with me about doing a story on Shadow and Daylight. They wanted to accompany them for half a year for this purpose. We decided to meet every fourteen days. Despite these relatively long breaks, I soon notice that the pups always recognize "their people." When they see them again, the pups first greet each individual and then relax, undisturbed by the camera, microphone, or cables. When substitutes replace the sound assistants once, however, the pups behave so shyly that the new personnel on the film team can only watch from a great distance if we are to work undisturbed at all.

A single stranger or new object can generate great uncertainty and

mistrust in the pups. The bulk of the filming takes place outside the park. This usually means a large expenditure, and many familiar people are needed to help. The more wolves take part, the more carefully planned everything must be. Even putting a collar and leash on them is difficult. Before every walk, great excitement rules in the enclosure; for the first happy yards of freedom, they pull so hard on the leash that it is almost impossible to hold them. So I require a guide for each one, someone whom the wolf absolutely trusts and has known since he was small. A wolf sometimes has preferences and often seeks out his person himself.

■ Relating to Females and Males

Interestingly, I have observed that in general the wolves form relationships with women much faster than with men. Maybe this is due to the gentler way females approach a wolf. During such encounters, a woman usually instinctively squats down (making herself smaller), stretches out an arm, speaks quietly to the wolf, and waits for it to come to her on its own. She offers wolves her friendship. A man, in contrast, doesn't make himself smaller. As a rule, he approaches the wolf with a certain dominance and tries to seize its friendship. Old Chinook reacted with great sensitivity to such behavior and required a seeming eternity before he would let himself be touched at all by a man. He could distinguish the sex of a visitor from a long distance.

In this matter, Daylight is the great exception in our pack. He has liked men since he was a pup. When a couple came to visit us, he greeted the woman very fleetingly but was very pleased about the male guest. At seven months old, while he still reacts with fear and much sensitivity to all strangers, Daylight forms a very deep friendship with one human acquaintance. On this day, we're filming a concluding scene for the wolf story outside the park, and the two meet each other. When the man visits the game park with his family fourteen days later and goes past the wolf enclosure, the young wolf recognizes him immediately, despite numerous other people in the area. While the rest of the pack remains quiet, Daylight runs back and forth along the fence and whimpers with happiness to see the man again. As the family finally moves on, Daylight howls

disappointedly after them for a long while. It is very moving to observe the intense emotions during every subsequent reunion.

Nanuk's preferences are somewhat more complex and peculiar. For reasons that are inexplicable to me, he prefers petite, plump women. One of my female friends, who certainly doesn't fit this description, has known the pack for a long time. She often goes with the wolves on our walks, helps with the filming, and visits the wolves in their enclosure. At first, she gets along best with Nanuk. During one walk, Nanuk happily jumps up on her over and over again. But once, as he lays his paws on her shoulders and licks her face, I notice his facial expression change and he quietly growls at the young woman. Before I can react, he drops down on all fours again and goes on his way. I can't explain his behavior and decide to keep an eye on it. At their next meeting, this occurs all over again: greeting, growling, walking away. To avoid deepening the tension between the two, I now keep Nanuk on a leash when we walk.

A couple of months later, I drive to see the wolves with my friend. She helps me bring the heavy plastic meat trough into the enclosure. I walk in front, unlock the gate, and as I step into the enclosure I notice a flash in Nanuk's eyes. I can barely close the door behind me to keep my friend outside. In the same instant, Nanuk shoots by me and jumps with

Shadow and Daylight walk side by side.

such force against the fence that the whole thing shakes. His clear body language and deep growling reveal that he is serious. I try to distract him with the food and am briefly successful. The wolves follow me and soon start to eat, but Daylight remains at the gate and pushes his nose through the fence to greet the woman who stayed behind. Nanuk notices this right away, lets his meat fall, reaches the pup within a few leaps, and pounces directly on him. The pup's scared cries and loud growls accompany this scene. Afterward, Daylight creeps away without turning back once. Nanuk's behavior clearly demonstrated that he no longer tolerates the young woman in the pack and strictly demands that all of the other family members join him.

I stand inside the enclosure and my friend is outside; between us there is a suddenly insurmountable barrier. We feel a certain sadness, because we both know that the wolf won't retract his decision.

It's difficult for humans to understand why something like this happens and exactly what the trigger for it could be. Life in a pack is very complicated. Wolves are forceful in their actions and the next attack could come without warning. Even when it's not easy, we must accept their decisions and respect their innate ways of behaving.

Epilogue

The pale January sun disappears beneath the horizon. I lean against an old spruce; the light fades. The frosty air creeps deeper and deeper into my limbs until it reaches my hands, dug deep in my pockets. I move my fingers, which are stiff with cold. I would so like to delay the time of departure.

The wolves lie resting in the middle of the enclosure. Snowflakes fall gently and blanket their sleeping bodies until soon they look like marble sculptures. Motionless, so as not to disturb the peaceful stillness, I enjoy the sight.

Wolves have fascinated me for a long time, but I would never have thought it possible that I could stand in the middle of a wolf pack and that they would play a large role in my life. I know that it is not completely natural to be accepted by them. With their instincts, strength, and speed, they are far superior to me, and to preserve our friendship I hope to correctly understand all of their signals and behavior.

All the wolves still live together, but soon Shadow and Daylight will leave the community of the white ones and move into their own enclosure. They're grown-up and independent; under the supervision of the adults, they've learned and practiced everything that is important for their future life. But the story goes on; new wolves will come. The little tundra wolf pack will soon get a new companion to take the place of Chinook, and Daylight and Shadow will not always be alone, either. Only when the two meet new wolf pups will it be clear whether

Opposite above: The new pack members are here: Ricco, Lobo, and Filou.

Opposite below: To be continued. . . .

140

they can summon the same care that they experienced from Flocke and Nanuk.

It gets dark. The cold becomes intolerable and it is just about time to go. But before I take the first step, the whole pack gets up and comes to me as if they sense that I will now leave them. I embrace one wolf after another, grasping them with both hands in their thick, warm fur and pulling them firmly against me to say good-bye. None of us knows what the next day will bring. Will they still accept me in the morning and tolerate me in their community? The pack accompanies me to the gate of the enclosure and silently watches me close it.

Even if my wolves can't follow the call of the wild, their existence here is very important. Through people's contact with living wolves in captivity, interest in the fate of wild wolves grows. And despite captivity, this pack also makes its own laws and remains independent, unruly, and always free inside.

Acknowledgments

This book could not have been written without the support and encouragement of friends, family, and many other helpers. I owe the following people special thanks:

Sabine Lutzmann and Thorge Huter, professional photographers and founders of the photo agency Fishing4 Network (www.fishing4.com), who have worked on this project with great care and patience for a year.

Bettina Kersten, who read my manuscript and helped me greatly with a first critique. Susanne Fischer-Rizzi and especially Rosemarie Kirschmann-Bartweiler, for their valuable suggestions and unmistakable knack for improvements.

Gisela Müller and Jörg Ahrend, who persistently accompanied me and the wolf pack on all our expeditions, often in fog, rain, wind, and cold.

Susanne Riedl (page 54, bottom) and Juliane Meyer (pages 32 and 141, top) for making their photographs available.

Not least, I thank Mr. Norbert Tietz, Director of the Lüneburger Heide Wild Game Park (www.wild-park.de), along with all of the park employees, who energetically supported me in my work and continue to do so.

Postscript

It is not so extraordinary to go for a walk one time with a wolf. Many friends of dogs know how happy they make their pets this way. The hand-reared wolves of the Lüneburger Heide Wild Game Park in Nindorf are also extremely happy when wolf mother Tanja Askani comes with the leash.

This is not an end in itself, but has far-reaching importance. Wolf researchers depend on practical experiences with wolves. Daily contact with various wolf species, from rearing to old age, helps. So this book reports in detail on contact with individual species, differences in temperament, and the various characters and needs of wolves. At this game park, we see our mission as providing visitors with as much information as possible about the lives of wolves, among other animals, to foster a better understanding of the wolf's uniqueness. Many patterns of behavior must be questioned to finally disprove the fairy tale of the evil wolf.

This task requires time and energy, and only continuing work will allow real, practice-based information about the wolf to be documented.

The Lüneburger Heide Wild Game Park in Nindorf thanks Tanja Askani for her extraordinary work and wishes this book—her second, by the way—much success.

Norbert Tietz
Director, Lüneburger Heide Wild Game Park